Dare to Dream

Work AND to Win

Dr. Tom Barrett

Dare to Dream AND Work to Win

Understanding the Dollars and Sense of Success in Network Marketing

Dr. Tom Barrett

To Linda, Lindsay, and Stephanie

You are the reason why I
dare to dream
and
work to win

CONTENTS

Acknowledgements

In network marketing no one succeeds alone. It is always a team effort. The same thing is true in writing a book. I am grateful for the team of people who have facilitated the completion of this book.

Rosetta Little - You may live 3000 miles away but you have been involved in every aspect of this writing. Your constant encouragement about the importance of this book kept me going when I was "lost in the fog."

Joel Goins, Dr. Bryan Grimmer, Frank and Danny Leonard, Jeff LeSourd, and Simon Warner - Entrepreneurs all. There were many moments when I drafted off of your vision for the completion of this book. It is my honor to be in this wonderful industry with you and to call you my friends.

Dr. Ron and Mary Seeley - Having done it, you both know what it takes to write a book. Thanks for standing by me in this endeavor. Your friendship has once again sustained me.

Hassell Wright - As an editor, your love of writing has made this a much better book. And your ability to laugh made the arduous task of manuscript review far more enjoyable.

Lindsay Barrett - Thanks for patiently helping your dad with technical support and computer graphics. Your computer skills amaze me.

Stephanie Barrett - Thanks for showing your dad how to do a "story web." I looked at your drawing every day when I sat down to write.

Linda Barrett - Your fingerprints are all over this book. Like my life, it is far better because of you. Thanks for your endless love and encouragement throughout this project.

To all of those on my team - Thank you for the privilege of dreaming and working with you. Let's keep winning together.

Introduction

Network marketing. As an industry it is here to stay. On Wall Street, in corporate board rooms, and in the general business community, network marketing is increasingly recognized as a primary means of transacting business. As a whole, these groups have been slow to embrace network marketing. But in today's business climate, they know it is a tremendous strategy for getting goods and services to the end line user - the customer. They know network marketing is extremely efficient, effective, and profitable.

These groups are not the only ones who were slow to accept network marketing as a legitimate and wise marketing concept. Countless individuals have heard about network marketing (or multi-level marketing) for years and have never taken it seriously.

I was one of those people. For years I had been exposed to various network marketing companies and had immediately dismissed all of them. Every time I heard of another company using this marketing strategy I assumed it was nothing more than a new variation of an old pyramid scheme. In my view, only a fool would get involved with network marketing.

After repeatedly meeting people whose lives and finances had been wonderfully changed through participation in network marketing, I decided to seriously examine this industry. I wanted to understand why these people were so highly motivated and incredibly excited. When I finished my research my thinking had changed 180 degrees. I concluded that I would be foolish *not to get involved* in this industry. I selected a company, jumped in, and got started. It was the wisest business decision I have ever made.

Network marketing will continue to attract unprecedented numbers of people in the upcoming years. This phenomenon will occur for two reasons:

1) Major changes have transformed the industry of network marketing. These changes are all positive. Network marketing has reached:

- new levels of integrity.
- new levels of professionalism.
- new levels of mainstream acceptability.
- new levels of profitability for participants.
- new levels of technological sophistication.
- new levels of training and support.

2) Major changes have transformed the traditional work force. Technological advancement and economic realities have created massive and permanent changes within numerous segments of the modern work world. The "rules of the game" have changed for anyone involved with law, medicine, general health care, sales, computers, small business, and countless other fields.

In the corporate arena, the aftermath of downsizing requires that smaller numbers of people produce greater volumes of work, in shorter periods of time, and with fewer resources. In the upper levels of corporate life, the law of supply and demand is a daily reality. The supply of individuals competing for the top positions exceeds the number of positions available.

For many people, life in the corporate world has become a game of musical chairs. While the music keeps playing, the people keep moving. But they all know that the music can stop at any moment. Consequently, they live in quiet, chronic fear that they will be the one left standing with no chair to sit in when the music stops.

The results of these changes are obvious. Many people in the current work world are concluding that:

- the time demands are too great.
- the stress is too high.
- the potential for freedom (of time and money) is too small.
- the hope of job security is gone.
- the rewards are too minimal.

These changes in the traditional work setting, along with the positive changes in network marketing, are creating the influx of new participants into network marketing.

If you are one of the people who is new to network marketing, let me welcome you to this wonderful world. My hope is that this book will shorten your learning curve, expand your vision, strengthen your resolve, and increase your likelihood of success. I have included many of the things that I wish I had heard about, or had understood, when I was beginning my business.

For you veterans of network marketing, this book will allow you to teach your downline many of the things you already know. You will also find much that is new or seldom addressed in network marketing.

For the sake of simplicity I have chosen to use the term "network marketing" throughout the book even though the term "multi-level marketing" would have been just as appropriate. Similarly, I have selected the term "rep" or "representative" to identify participants in network marketing. If you, or your organization, use the word "distributor" instead of "rep" please know that I am using this term to include you as well.

Whether you are new or experienced in network marketing, my desire is for this book to assist you in the growth of your business. Network marketing is the ideal place for those special individuals who dare to dream and work to win. May this book help you do both.

—Tom Barrett, Ph.D.

Dare to Dream
AND
Work to Win

Part One:

FOUNDATIONS FOR SUCCESS

CHAPTER ONE

SEEING THROUGH
THE FOG

L ondon, England. It is known as the city of "pea-soup fog." The fog is so thick it impairs vision, muffles sound, and slows the progress of those enveloped in it. For many of us, network marketing could be called the industry of pea-soup fog. From a distance, people correctly see that network marketing (or multilevel marketing) is a bright and exciting world that enhances vision and lifts the spirit. It is a world which welcomes all people to come, and once there, to dream as big as they dare, work harder than they have ever worked, and taste a freedom that they didn't think possible. It is a great place to live and work.

For many participants in network marketing, this industry which looks so bright and attractive from a distance, becomes enveloped in fog after we enter it. It is easy to lose our vision, not hear what is being said by others, and see our progress slow to a crawl.

Maybe you know this fog as well as I do. I got lost in it. I spent my first year lost in the fog of network marketing. I knew this was a business in which the average person with above-average desire could succeed. I had met too many ordinary people in network marketing making extraordinary sums of money. But network marketing wasn't clicking for me. The growth of my business seemed modest and average. In fact, it seemed slow. Too slow. But, lost in the fog, I could not understand why. I was working the business as well as I knew how.

The only thing that kept me going was my unflinching conviction that the merger of network marketing with

> **"You can work your business full-time or part-time, but not spare-time."**

high-quality companies was a winning combination for the company, customers, and the representatives or distributors. But I was still waiting for this conviction to translate into personal experience. I did not want to hear of one more person in network marketing who was doing phenomenally well. Others' success stories were becoming two-edged swords for me. The stories simultaneously motivated and frustrated me. I wanted my own success. I sensed there was something that I was not understanding or doing. I was missing something. But, never having been in network marketing, I had no idea what it might be. I could not see through the fog. And until it lifted, there was little that I could do but to keep working this business to the best of my ability.

Eventually, the fog began to lift. I was no longer just looking. I began to see. I had survived the network marketing learning curve. I knew that my business would thrive because I had begun to understand and implement some of the core concepts of growing a large, successful network marketing business. Knowing these things has allowed me to settle into this endeavor with vigor, patience, and confidence.

When the fog vanished, three foundational principles of network marketing emerged. Many people in network marketing have never heard of them. Some of us have heard of them but we pay no attention. We dismiss these principles as simple suggestions, clichés, or random ideas. Consequently, the importance of these concepts as bedrock principles is lost. Like most "simple ideas," there is a wealth of insight buried within them. The three foundational principles of network marketing are:

1. CONSISTENT EFFORT
2. DUPLICATION
3. GIVE IT ENOUGH TIME

Let's explore these principles one at a time. While they may look innocuous, they are imperative for sustained focus and success in our network marketing businesses.

PRINCIPLE #1: CONSISTENT EFFORT

Imagine someone's attempting to lose twenty pounds and wanting to get into great physical shape. Now imagine that they are attempting to decide between two strategies. In one strategy, they eat moderately and exercise each day. The other strategy would allow them to eat as they pleased each day and not have to exercise. But every seventh day, they would have to abstain from food, run five miles, and lift weights for two hours. Which strategy would you recommend? Or, imagine someone's wanting to become an accomplished musician. Would you recommend that they practice for 30 minutes a day or one day a week for three hours?

The answer to these questions is obvious. The principle of consistent effort is not difficult to understand as a general concept in life. Its difficulty lies in its implementation. For those of us who expect to succeed in network marketing, this general concept has to be applied specifically to growing our businesses.

We have to be willing to give consistent chunks of time to our businesses if we are serious about their growth. The size of the time allotments may vary based on our goals and other life factors. But without regular, consistent time put into our businesses on a daily basis, they are not likely to grow. This consistent time is necessary whether the goal is to create $300, $3,000, or $300,000 per month. Following are some practical and psychological ideas to keep in mind when pursuing consistent effort:

Discipline Is the Price of Success

Success, greatness, and character do not come from one grand moment. They are honed and sharpened in the quiet and obscure moments of each day. They come from doing many little, boring, and seemingly irrelevant things one at a time. The quiet, cumulative effect of these is success. In network marketing, that means one more two-minute phone call to inquire about someone's interest, one more breakfast or cup of coffee with someone to show the business presentation, one more fax, follow-up call, training, etc. As stand-alone incidents, they are barely noteworthy. But collectively, they create focus, cultivate character, increase skill sets, and grow a team of like-minded winners.

You Can Work Your Business Full-Time or Part-Time, But Not Spare-Time

The reason for this is simple. None of us have any spare time. We were using twenty-four hours per day long before we ever heard of network marketing. And we will continue to. The only way people will have time for their businesses is to make time. Network marketing is a business of inconvenience. People are not sitting around with gaps in their schedules waiting for them to be filled.

Build Your Business in the "Nooks and Crannies"

Do you remember the old Thomas' English Muffin commercials? They used to refer to the "nooks and crannies" of their muffins. I recommend that reps grow their businesses in the nooks and crannies of daily life. This is how I grew the bulk of my business. In my private practice, I have ten minutes free between clients. That is a nook, or if you prefer, a cranny. Many of my appointments for my network marketing business are made during this free time between client appointments. (By the way, when you call people, and they know that you literally have only a minute or two, they are not going to expect you to give them a lot of details over the phone. They allow me to get right to the point, set up the appointment, and get off the phone.) Additionally, many of my appointments are set up while I am in my car driving from my office to Capitol Hill. (And again, when I am on my car phone, people do not expect me to spend extended time on the phone.)

What are the nooks and crannies of your life? When do they occur? How long do they last? What parts of your days do you fill with small talk and insignificant activities when you could be growing your business? What do you do that is momentarily pleasant but ultimately un-

> *"When someone says they do not have time for something, they have stated a priority, not a fact."*

productive? Could this time be spent growing your business, reaching your goal, and changing your life? Everyone has some daily life nooks and crannies. What separates the winners from the wishers in network marketing is how these times are used. The following expression is absolutely true: *When someone says they do not have time for something, they have not stated a fact. They have simply stated a priority.*

In Network Marketing, a Pack Horse Is Better Than a Race Horse

Reps make two common mistakes in network marketing. They think they need to be a race horse that is lightning fast so they can "tear this thing up." Or, they think they need to find a race horse that will become the next superstar in their company. I no longer want to be a race horse, and I do not want to look for race horses. I have seen too many of them. They may look fabulous in the stall, at the starting gate, and running a half-mile track. But they don't have the stamina for anything other than a sprint. Success in network marketing is not about being a race horse. It is all about being a pack horse.

A pack horse will not impress you with its speed or appearance. But it will amaze you with its quiet strength, patience, and stamina. Like the Energizer Bunny, it just keeps going and going and going. This is what growing any business requires. And growing a network marketing business is no exception. It requires consistent effort. Sustained focus. When you listen to the people who are making large sums in network marketing, you will find they make it not because they are flashy race horses. They are pack horses, individuals who dared to dream, and then they set out to pursue their dreams one moment, one phone call, one appointment, one meeting, at a time. Nook and cranny after nook and cranny. And their moods, motivations, the weather, or *TV Guide* did not determine what they would do. They merged their dream with determination. They set some goals and then set out to reach them. They did a little every day. They sustained focus. They gave consistent effort. Today, we honor them as heroes. And they are. They applied a concept that is simple to understand and difficult to implement: consistent effort.

PRINCIPLE #2: DUPLICATION

Duplication. This principle eluded me my first year in network marketing. I was not opposed to it. I understood it as a general concept, like simple-cell division. And, like many others, I quoted America's first billionaire, J. Paul Getty, who stated, "I would rather have one percent of the efforts of one hundred men working for me rather than one hundred percent of my own efforts." But the vital truth hidden in this principle did not hit me until I began to be frustrated and fatigued by slow growth in my organization. It occurred to me that "the buck stopped with me." Literally. I did not know how to create ongoing duplication in my team. Until I learned this, I was going to remain stuck and generating only a few thousand dollars per month. And I knew that was chump change compared to what was available.

I began to study the people who were growing large teams. There was one common denominator among them: duplication. They were all using a simple, systematic method to grow their teams. And the genius of their success lay in its simplicity because simple is duplicable.

> *"Grow your business*
>
> *in the nooks and*
>
> *crannies of your*
>
> *daily life."*

Understanding the mathematical power of duplication is compelling. And it should be. This is not a concept that works in theory but not in practical reality. On the contrary, duplication is much more attainable than most people realize. But only if they know HOW to first create and then to sustain duplication.

Pretend that you are in your first month in your network marketing business. What will happen if you, as a rep, sign up one other representative the first month? The next month, both of you do the same thing. If you consistently repeat this simple process for twelve months with no one ever sponsoring more than one person a month, what will happen? The numbers speak for themselves.

THE MATHEMATICAL POWER OF SIMPLE DUPLICATION

Month 1: You + 1 = 2	Month 7: 64 + 64 = 128
Month 2: 2 + 2 = 4	Month 8: 128 + 128 = 256
Month 3: 4 + 4 = 8	Month 9: 256 + 256 = 512
Month 4: 8 + 8 = 16	Month 10: 512 + 512 = 1024
Month 5: 16 + 16 = 32	Month 11: 1024 + 1024 = 2048
Month 6: 32 + 32 = 64	Month 12: 2048 + 2048 = 4096

Imagine sponsoring only one person per month, training that person to do likewise, and having more than four thousand people in your organization at the end of twelve months. People commonly have two reactions to seeing these numbers. The first is amazement; they are shocked to see the power of exponential growth laid out before them. Like compounding interest–where the value of your money starts and where it ends up are very different. The second reaction is to begin to doubt that this could actually happen in their own businesses. So, like many people do with compounding interest, they ignore the practical, life-changing power of this concept.

Those who respect the power of exponential growth realize that it will allow them to leverage two of life's most important commodities: time and money. They begin seeking a way to make this mathematical concept approximate the reality of their own organizational growth. This exponential growth and its life-changing consequences are most likely to occur when reps understand that there is an invisible infrastructure in successful network marketing teams.

How Does This "Thing" Really Work?

Do you ever wonder how wealth is actually achieved in network marketing? Do you wonder how it really works? For me, as a researcher and business analyst, it is important to understand *how* and *why* things work. Following is my view of the invisible infrastructure that holds a large successful network marketing team together. This infrastructure, when developed over time, is what creates wealth.

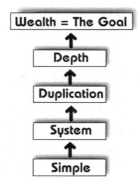

The invisible infrastructure that creates
wealth in network marketing

Let's see how the progression and logic of this infrastructure fit together. At the start, network marketing must be kept very *simple*. In its purest form, it is really just gathering customers of our products or services and some other representatives (or customer gatherers). This is the essence of what we do. Sometimes veterans forget that doing this is not as "simple" as it appears. Having a *system* is what allows us to give new participants direction and support. A system, or "tracks to run on," allows them to *duplicate* with others precisely what we have modeled to them. Over time, this results in large numbers of people who are each going out and getting a few more customers and "customer gatherers." This is what creates *depth* in an organization. And ongoing depth is what yields *wealth*. Let's briefly examine each component of this infrastructure.

SIMPLE

Simplicity. It is the cornerstone upon which everything else is built. It is the starting point. It means what many of the leaders in the industry say repeatedly: "Keep your business uncomplicated. Basic. Fun." There is genius hidden in their counsel.

Embarrassed by Simplicity

But many newcomers to network marketing, especially professionals, blow right past this principle. We miss the genius of simplicity. To us simple looks...well...too simple. It is not sophisticated enough. It lacks class. It is not professional. There is no polish. No pizazz. So, we get involved and quietly tell ourselves that we will do this thing called network marketing, but we will buff it up so that we are not so embarrassed. We will move our company and network marketing to a higher level. We will bring it up to our professional standards rather than lower ourselves to such pedestrian simplicity.

So with enough business acumen to see opportunity, we get involved. And with a large dose of professional arrogance (which is really a euphemism for professional ignorance), we condescend to affiliating with network marketing. But secretly, we are eager to dress it up, clean it up, and make it more impressive. In doing this, we quickly do two things: We demonstrate our ignorance, and we kill any chance of creating wealth. *Wealth is only possible if we keep things so simple that they are totally duplicable.* Those who do this will become wealthy. Those who do not will become weary.

SYSTEM

In network marketing, a system is a means of teaching people a simple, methodical way of growing a business. It is giving them tracks to run on. A road map. It provides participants some direction so that they know *what* to do next and *how* to do it. It helps them to effectively focus their energy and motivation on two essential things that we do in network marketing: gather a few reps and teach them how to systematically duplicate this same process over and over again.

People Need to Plug Into the System

Joel Goins is one of the finest trainers in network marketing. He has the best insights and instincts of anyone I have ever met when it comes to understanding people and network marketing. In many ways, he is my mentor in this industry. He has repeatedly stated, *"People need to plug into the system."* When I first heard him say this, I didn't object. I would nod, vaguely understand what he said, and move on. Little did I understand that he was trying to convey to me one of the most pivotal aspects of the business. I had no idea that literal fortunes were won or lost here.

I eventually comprehended that without a system to follow, many people in network marketing are like a powerful locomotive engine that has no tracks to run on. They get bogged down and go nowhere. They begin with wonderful motivation and vision, but because they lack a systematic method of growing a team and creating revenue, they become discouraged and watch their energy, enthusiasm, and hope begin to dissipate. These people often assume that something is lacking in them that prevents success. In reality, the only thing they are missing is a systematic method of growing their businesses.

DUPLICATION AND DEPTH

Depth is created when people sign up new reps and help those reps go out and sign up others, who then go out and do the same thing. The more successfully this process of duplication is repeated, the more this creates depth, and in turn, wealth. Thinking in generational or genealogical terms, when someone sponsors a new rep, they are like a parent who just gave birth to a child - the next generation. When this child has children, the original parents now have grandchildren. Depth occurs when reps (the parents) begin to see their offspring create children and great grandchildren, etc. Until our offspring start "multiplying like rabbits," depth will not be achieved. It looks like this:

You (the parent)

Your personally sponsored rep (your child)

Their personally sponsored rep (your grandchild)

Their personally sponsored rep (your great grandchild)

It is always gratifying to hear when a rep sponsors another rep. But someone signing up another rep tells us very little. *It is time to get excited when a rep you bring in has great grandchildren of his or her own.* Now you are onto something. This generational depth is the sign of life and energy in your organization. It is the sign that people are coming into your business, are well trained and supported, and then are going out and repeating that same process. That creates wealth.

Connecting the Dots

Focusing on a simple and systematic method of growing a team creates duplication and depth. As these occur, wealth begins to be achieved. (Note the paradox: When we focus on wealth alone, it will not be achieved in network marketing. But if we will focus on duplication, helping others succeed, and putting a system in place that increases the likelihood of others' successes, then we will almost inadvertently reach our own goal of wealth. Sometimes, the bull's-eye is hit by aiming in the opposite direction.)

PRINCIPLE # 3: GIVE IT ENOUGH TIME

When was the last time you attempted a simple repair job on something in your home or your car? The task appeared simple and doable. You estimated how much time, energy, and money the repair would require. (In the end, we often discover that these "simple projects" are larger than expected and that our initial estimates were not accurate.)

Growing a large network marketing business is somewhat like this. The task is bigger than we imagined. (Fortunately, so is the return on our investment.) It is the third principle that reminds us to be patient. Settle in, take the long view, and stay on-task. Remember to give it enough time.

This principle, like the first one of consistent effort, is not difficult to understand. But I have never been in an industry where people have more warped expectations and serious time distortion than they do in network marketing. At times, there is very little realism. Throughout this book, I hope to inject some. Realism does not discourage people; it sets them free. It allows them to settle in for the intermediate and long haul.

Without a dose of realism, people get started with false expectations. When their businesses grow more slowly than anticipated, they conclude that either this business does not work or that it will not work for them. The first conclusion is a general one about the industry of network marketing as a whole. The other is a specific conclusion about themselves...that they are not capable of succeeding in this endeavor. In either case, their erroneous conclusions cause them to remove themselves from growing their businesses. Sometimes this is a formal exit. But most of the time, it is death by neglect. They simply do nothing to feed and grow their businesses. They let them languish until it is time to pay some normal business expense. Then they decide to pull the plug.

Be Patient

The rest of this book will help you understand why we have to "give it enough time." It takes time, significant periods of time, to grow a network marketing business with depth and duplication. It takes time to start as a new rep and then to achieve the leadership positions that are available. It takes time to move from the goal of wealth to understanding the means of attaining wealth. It takes time to understand the invisible learning curve and skill sets required to do this business.

Additionally, each individual comes into his or her network marketing business with a personal learning curve. It may be learning how network marketing works; it may be learning to trust oneself as a leader or a servant of others; or, it may take time to truly comprehend how big this industry is and that it is the invitation of a lifetime. Whatever a rep's learning curve is, he or she needs more time than anticipated to get through it. It is important to face this reality and then keep moving.

This principle of "give it enough time" is generally suggested as a time period. Usually, it turns out to mean from the time we join as a new rep to the time when our business is generating significant revenue. I agree with this measurement of time.

Give Enough Time Each Day and Each Week

But let's look at this "give it enough time" idea from another perspective. *If our business is going to grow significantly over time, we need to be giving it enough time on a daily and a weekly basis.* If we are not doing this, it is improbable that our business will grow, no matter how many months or years we have been registered as a rep.

When interacting with others in network marketing, I am not as interested in how long someone has been signed up with their company as I am in how many hours he or she has logged working their business. Signing up for the business means nothing. Working the business means everything.

Measuring Time Like Pilots

It would be interesting in an industry like network marketing, where everyone is an independent representative, if we kept track of time like pilots do. When they want to ascertain how long or how seriously someone has been a pilot, they do not ask, "How long have you been flying?" or "How long have you been a pilot?" They don't care when someone became interested in flying, how many classes and seminars they have attended, how much they know about the physics of flight, or how well they have studied aviation manuals. And they don't really care when the person registered for a flight class. Pilots only want to know one thing: "How many hours have you logged flying?" They only need to know how many hours you have sat in the cockpit and flown a plane. The answer says it all. There is a vast difference between an individual who has flown fifteen hours and one who has logged fifteen thousand hours!

In network marketing, there is only one thing that counts as hours logged or flight time: Showing your business presentation to someone. Period. That's it. This is a person-to-person, face-to-face business. And if we are not getting the business presentation in front of other people, then we are not logging flight time. We may fancy ourselves as pilots, we may read the monthly pilots' magazine, we may watch videos, go to seminars and weekly pilots' meetings. But none of these count as flying. In reality, we are going nowhere. It is all make-believe motion.

Maybe that is why Rosetta Little, one of network marketing's top income earners, and one of my heroes, says, *"He or she who shows the most business presentations wins."* She knows nothing else will grow a large team.

Realistic Expectations and False Pressures

If we learned to think like pilots in terms of "hours logged," it would bring much more realism to the expectations some reps have. It would also reduce a lot of false pressure that others have.

Think of the thousands of people in network marketing companies who honestly have only three or four hours a week to grow their businesses. They are legitimately busy with other priorities in their lives. They often compare themselves to someone who has been signed up for about the same amount of time but who has many more hours to devote to their business each week. This comparison is unfair, and it will only make the rep working the business on a part-time basis feel like a failure even though he or she may be doing a very good job. It is much more realistic to evaluate the growth rate of a business by the number of hours logged. This sets a rep free from the curse of false comparison.

> **"Success is not about being a race horse. It is about being a pack horse."**

On the other hand, there are people in network marketing who live with wild expectations. They thought all they had to do to become wealthy was to sign a form, work a little, and then wait. These are the individuals who would be most helped by forgetting when they signed up to affiliate with a company. These reps would better serve themselves by asking only one question: "How many hours of flight time have I logged in my business?" Many of them would be shocked to discover that they have only logged a few hours of flight over an extended period of time! And yet they wonder why their business "is not taking off." *If you are not logging steadily increasing amounts of flight time, then there is no point in acting dismayed when your business is not reaching a point of liftoff. One will not happen without the other.*

A Checklist for Reality

These three principles of network marketing (consistent effort, duplication, and give it enough time) allow you to ask questions that provide a checklist for reality. Are you giving consistent effort to your business? Or is your effort sporadic and catch-as-catch-can? Are you seeing duplication in your business? Do you know what "duplication" is in network marketing? Do you see why it is of paramount importance? Do you know how to create and sustain duplication? And finally, do you have realistic financial expectations? Have you logged many hours of flight time? How many? What is keeping you from logging more hours? Is it time, skill, fear, stalling, or something else? If you think this opportunity is real, what is keeping you from taking advantage of it to the best of your ability?

While waiting for the fog to lift so that you can "see" what you are doing in your business, there are some other things you can concentrate on. They are guaranteed to keep you on course even if you feel like you are flying blind. The first of these is to recognize that success is no accident.

CHAPTER TWO

SUCCESS:
IT'S NO ACCIDENT

I'm not sure when or how, but somewhere along the way, it became a habit. Now I do it unconsciously each time I leave my home. I go through a quick mental check list to be sure I didn't forget anything. Usually I pause for a moment and think, "Let's see, do I have my wallet, my car keys, money, schedule...?" You probably do something like this too.

What amazes me are the millions of people who leave their homes and remember all the little, incidental things that will allow them to get through the day, but forget the one big thing that puts their day in perspective: their dreams.

Dreams allow you to envision future realities. They enrich your life, not by giving it false hope, but by giving it realistic hope that results in energy, passion, and direction. People who live with the ability to see a future that is based in reality, full of hope, and eagerly awaited, are the wealthiest of all. One of the great privileges of working with people in network marketing is that they are individuals who have dreams. For many of these people, every day is another shot at making their dreams become a reality.

Why do dreams become a reality for some, while for others their dreams end up relegated to the discard pile of old wishes that never materialized? Why will network marketing become all that some people expected, while for others it will not pan out? The answers lie in the beliefs, attitudes, insights, and skills of each individual. The remainder of this book will deal with these factors. Additionally, there are some practical points which profoundly determine a person's success in network marketing. They are unassumingly called "the four ingredients for success." They are vitally important, and I am grateful to my dear friend, Joel Goins, for having taught them to me.

I suggest that you make these four ingredients for success the foundation upon which you build your business. Memorize them. Know them cold. Then live and teach them. They serve as anchors that tether you and your team to reality when the going gets tough. Almost without fail, when people are successful in network marketing, they are applying these ingredients. Similarly, when I watch people bail out of this industry, I know they have not integrated these suggestions into the warp and woof of their businesses, and consequently, their dreams have unraveled.

THE FOUR INGREDIENTS FOR SUCCESS

1. DETERMINE WHAT YOU WANT.
2. DECIDE WHAT YOU ARE WILLING TO RESCHEDULE OR GIVE UP IN ORDER TO GET WHAT YOU WANT.
3. ASSOCIATE WITH PEOPLE WHO WILL HELP YOU GET WHAT YOU WANT.
4. HAVE A PLAN THAT WORKS; WORK YOUR PLAN.

Don't be fooled by the fact that these ingredients don't look very exciting. They are what will keep you excited about growing your business. In this chapter, let's consider the first two ingredients for success.

INGREDIENT #1: DETERMINE WHAT YOU WANT

Dan O'Brien tells the story of sitting in a meeting with other Olympic hopefuls a couple of years before the games were held. Addressing the athletes was a former decathlon winner who asked how many of them had specific goals for their Olympic dreams. Everyone raised a hand. Then the speaker asked how many had these goals written down. Almost every athlete raised a hand. Then he asked a final question: how many had their written goals with them? No one raised a hand. Not a single athlete had brought written goals. From then on, Dan O'Brien carried his goals with him everyday and everywhere. He went on to win the decathlon gold medal.

Be absolutely clear about what you want out of your business before you decide what you will put into it. Why is this so important? Because goals create focus, energy, and passion. They strengthen the will. They create purposeful living, and they become a compass which gives us our headings when we get lost in the fog. Goals keep us on track when the task seems too big, too difficult, and too far away. When our dreams and future goals are vivid, it is much easier to know how to schedule our lives in the present.

In any significant life endeavor, there will be moments when we experience fatigue, frustration, and doubt. In those moments we are acutely aware of what we are doing, how exacting it is, and how much easier it would be to quit. So much discomfort could be eliminated by just quitting. And in those moments when we are tempted to

25

take the easy way out, we will ask ourselves, "Why am I doing this?" It is a good question. But when we ask this question, we'd better have a reply that is quick, cogent, and unequivocating.

For this reason, knowing *why* we do this business is more important than *how* we do it. The *why* is what keeps us going while we learn the *how* of the business. Ask any entrepreneur what keeps him or her going when business is not developing as swiftly as they imagined. There is only one thing that keeps them going: the clarity of their dreams. They keep their eyes on the prize. They take the long view. They don't let their immediate circumstances rob them of their future dreams. Or, as Paul Orberson (who makes more than $1 million per month in this industry) reminds us, "Don't let the bugs on the windshield rob you of seeing the horizon." It is a vivid, palpable conviction of the future that keeps people going when the present is not all that pleasant. They have determined what they want. And now they will not be denied. Deciding what they want and why they want it creates what Bear Bryant called "bulldog tenacity." A clear dream does two things: it creates perspective and perseverance.

Network Marketing: The Ultimate Utility Vehicle

When was the last time you went out just to sit in your car? You had nowhere to go, but you decided to spend several hours just hanging out in your parked car. My guess is that it has probably been quite a while since you did this. (Unless one of your reasons for growing a business was to purchase the car of your dreams, and you have just gone out and purchased it!) Why don't we do this? Because we use our cars to get us from one place to another. If we have nowhere to go, or we want to stay where we are, then there is no point in getting into an automobile.

The same thing is true of the network marketing business. In utilitarian terms, it is nothing more than a vehicle to get us from one place in life to another. It looks like this:

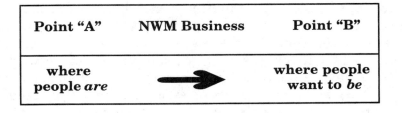

Point "A"	NWM Business	Point "B"
where people *are*	➡	where people want to *be*

A network marketing business is a vehicle for change.

People will get involved with network marketing when they recognize it is a fabulous means of transportation to create movement in their lives. When they are absolutely clear about where they are in life, why they want to leave where they are, and where they ultimately want to go, *then* they see the value of getting into network marketing. It now serves a purpose for them. But until they envision network marketing as a vehicle that creates movement, they see no point in getting involved with it. When talking to people about this industry, I always tell them, "If you don't have a dream, and if you have no real desire to see your life circumstances change, then don't bother getting involved with network marketing. This is a business only for those fortunate people who still have a dream."

So why are you involved with network marketing? Or, why are you considering getting involved? What do you want out of it? What would make the hard work worthwhile? I suggest that you take time right now and reflect on your reasons for affiliating with network marketing. Make your goals as specific, vivid, and real as you can. Write them down, and then make several copies.

One copy is for you to carry at all times. That way you can always answer your own question when you demand to know "why am I doing this?" A second copy is to give to the person who brought you into the business. When you want to blow them off and ignore their suggestions for staying committed to growing your business, they can pull out your list of what you want and gently remind you that there are some very important, real, and personal reasons that got you started in network marketing. If the reasons were strong enough to get you started, they might be strong enough to keep you going. Lastly, give a list to the people about whom you care the most. Usually, people are not involved in network marketing for self-serving reasons. They are doing this for people they love and care about...spouse, children, siblings, parents, etc. When the relational pain of growing a business is felt, it can be helpful to remind each other of shared dreams and the desire to change the future by the hard work being done today.

INGREDIENT #2: DECIDE WHAT YOU ARE WILLING TO RESCHEDULE OR GIVE UP IN ORDER TO GET WHAT YOU WANT

Have you ever seen a country dog that chases every car that comes along? It waits in the front yard, spots a car coming down the road, and jumps up to meet it. Then it runs alongside the car as fast as it can while barking so fiercely that the driver is inclined to drive a little faster and secretly pray that the car doesn't break down. Have you ever wondered what the dog would do if it actually caught the car? What would it do if it managed to sink its teeth into the bumper? My guess is that while it may have spent its life chasing cars, it would have no idea what to do if it actually caught one!

> **"Be clear about what you want out of your business before you decide what you will put into it."**

Watching some people in network marketing is like watching the country dog. They have spent their lives waiting for something that could literally change their entire financial futures. They wish they could be the boss, set their own schedules, get paid what they are worth, grow their own businesses, not be told what to do, and for once be able to test their limits to see how good they could really be. If only they could get a chance... If only they could find a vehicle for freedom that they could sink their teeth into... Guess what...in network marketing, the dog has caught the car.

When the Dog Catches the Car

And now that the car has been caught, and the vehicle to personal and monetary freedom found, people have to decide what to do with it. It is time to stop chasing and start doing. Stop wishing and start working. Stop making excuses and start making it happen. It is a huge mental transition to move from living at the beck and call of your job or boss to learning to live in a manner that is based on your own values, dreams, and internal desires. Many people have literally spent their lives being told what to do, when to do it, and how to do it. The thought of living by internal motivation, personal choice, and not by the dictates of some external source, disorients them. Many are overwhelmed at the beauty of this freedom. Some realize they lack the internal fortitude and drive necessary to manage this freedom. They don't know how to live without someone else being their boss. They will respond to someone else telling them what to do (external motivation), but they don't know how to motivate themselves enough to "get off the dime" (internal motivation) and take charge of their futures, their finances, and their lives.

So the second ingredient for success reveals if someone has what it takes to be a player in network marketing. It will tell you much about the strength of their dreams, their desire for change, the depth of their character, the strength of their will, and their understanding of how life changing involvement in this industry can be. Additionally, it will reveal a rep's ability to focus and the rep's willingness to pay a price for success. (Later, we will discuss how being willing to reschedule or give up something in order to achieve a cherished goal will further reveal a rep's core beliefs about the world and his or her place in it.)

How can this second ingredient reveal so much so quickly? Because it is the rubicon which must be crossed. If a rep is not willing to pay a price for success, will not submit to self-discipline in order to turn dreams into reality, and will not work to become a winner, then he or she does not have what it takes to make future dreams become present reality. The second ingredient is true about life, not just success in network marketing.

The First Lesson for New Reps

Many of us who have become reps and are able to see the magnitude of this opportunity in network marketing get genuinely excited about what it will mean to our futures. And we see it so clearly that we get excited about what it can mean for others' futures...if they would get involved. Out of genuine enthusiasm and love, we encourage and exhort them to get involved with us. We want this to work for them too. But this sets us up for one of the first difficult lessons most of us have to learn in network marketing: *You cannot want this business for people more than they want it for themselves.* Others cannot draft off of our vision. They will only get going and keep moving if they have their own dreams and sufficient internal desire to do what it takes to make their dreams come true. You have honored them with the invitation to associate with you in growing a business that could generate more revenue

> *"Knowing why we do this business is more important than how we do this business."*

enue in a month than they ever imagined earning in a year. But until they envision it themselves, appreciate it, and desire it, you are wasting your time. They will feel like dead weight as you try to "drag them along" in the business. Leave them alone. Move on. Go work with someone else. When they are motivated to take responsibility for their own life dreams, then you can assist, serve, support, and teach them as much as you want.

The Price of Admission Versus the Price of Success

Countless people will express interest in something that can be as life-changing as network marketing. They will be intrigued, curious, and tempted to say "yes" to your offer of helping them get what they purport to want out of life. But in the final moment, they will decline active involvement. What is it that will keep them out of the winners' circle? It will not be the price of admission; it is the price of success. They love *the idea* of growing a business, being independently wealthy, having money to give away, etc. But while they love to think of these things, they gag on *the effort* required to make them happen. The thought of missing their favorite TV show, a tee time, hunting season, or some social gathering is unthinkable to them. So they cling to the routine and minor events of their lives and casually let go of their dreams. It occurs so subtly that they never realize what they have done. (For example, millions of people literally plan their weekly schedules around shows like *Frasier, Seinfeld, or Home Improvement*. This scheduling creates the illusion of structure, focus, and purpose in their lives. It never dawns on the viewers that the actors they are watching are living their own dreams. But the price of watching the actors live their dreams is the neglect of the viewers' dreams!)

These same people will have some faint regrets when they see network marketing changing your life and not theirs. But they will quickly dismiss their remorse and conclude that you really got lucky. It will not occur to them that your business worked for you because you worked your business. You decided what you wanted, and then you decided what you were willing to give up or reschedule in order to get what you wanted.

These first two ingredients for success (determine what you want and decide what you are willing to reschedule or give up in order to get what you want) are extremely important. Dreams create hope. Goals create focus. And focus creates fuel that propels us to action. Why did you get involved with network marketing? Where do you want it to take you? What do you want out of it? How would you like your life to be different because of it? And what are you willing to do to make what you want become reality?

Sometimes we hold the answers to our prayers in our own hands.

CHAPTER
THREE

INSPIRED
BY OTHERS

Network marketing participants are independent
representatives in a business and legal sense. They
are free to grow their businesses as they choose
as long as they do it in a manner that reflects the
standards and policies of their companies. But independent does not mean alone. Your network marketing business will grow larger and faster if you are a team player
and understand the value of association. This is what
makes the third ingredient for success so important.

INGREDIENT #3: ASSOCIATE WITH PEOPLE WHO
WILL HELP YOU GET WHAT YOU WANT

King Solomon wrote, "He who walks with wise men becomes wise, while the companion of fools will suffer harm."
What was he writing about? He understood that others

impact our lives. For better or worse, they "rub off on us." We become like those with whom we associate. That is why we caution our children to choose their friends wisely. We already understand this life principle. We need to understand how this principle is vital to our success in network marketing. No matter how individually committed we are to success, we cannot do this business alone. Obviously, we cannot earn serious residual income without others. We cannot get promoted to the more lucrative leadership positions without others. We cannot build a huge, national or international team that is ever-increasing in size and revenues without others. From start to finish, this is a team business. It is a people business. We all get to dream, build, and win together.

What makes association such an important component of success? Through the power of association we stay focused, energized, and excited. The beliefs of others impact our own beliefs. Their courage, optimism, and tenacity rub off on us. Association with others can inspire us to new levels of personal vision and determination.

Positively Infected by Others

Have you ever been around people who have expectant, positive, unshakable attitudes? Such attitudes are like air-borne viruses. They are extremely contagious. You cannot be with these people for extended periods without "catching" some of what they have. Their "infectious disease" creates symptoms of joy, hope, wisdom, fortitude, and a strong work ethic. Like "Typhoid Mary," they impact people wherever they go. Except, in this case, what they leave behind them are lives that have been positively impacted. There is no need to hope that our immune system is strong enough to resist what they expose us to.

Negative Infections

On the other hand, the immune system of our beliefs and attitudes is exposed every day to heavy doses of doubt, disbelief, and cynicism...cynicism about life in general and opportunity in particular. When new reps get started in network marketing, they will begin interacting with others about their lives, dreams, goals, and needs. The reps will then attempt to articulate to those people how network marketing will dovetail with what they want out of life.

> "A clear dream does two things: it creates perspective and perseverance."

Several things will quickly astonish new reps. First, they will be amazed at the large number of people who have abandoned all serious expectations that their life dreams can ever be achieved. Second, new reps will be amazed at the common misconception others have about network marketing. Those perceptions are often thirty years behind the times. When I meet someone like this, I ask them if they have a rotary phone and a party line instead of a private line. When they respond "no," I suggest to them that their knowledge of network marketing is thirty years behind the times. Like our modern day phones, network marketing is not what it used to be. It is much more sophisticated and is becoming a primary and indispensable means of transacting business.

35

Often, an enthusiastic rep keeps bumping into individuals who have no dreams, have antiquated views of network marketing, and have no grasp of what affiliation with a high-quality network marketing company could mean to his or her life. When this happens, a rep can get discouraged. This is normal and understandable. Overexposure to these negative individuals can easily result in infection. It is at this juncture that the power of association is so important.

Mama Said There Would Be Days Like This

Association with others who are clearly focused and highly motivated will keep you going when your will is weak, your vision dim, your mind weary, and your heart tired. And every person, no matter how great a leader, no matter how internally motivated, will have moments like this. Do you remember the song, "Mama Said There Would Be Days Like This"? In growing any business, including a network marketing business, there will be times when:

- you question your sanity while waiting for this thing to take off.

- others question your sanity for waiting so long and working so hard.

- you doubt if you have the stamina and skill to see the job through.

- you doubt that you will ever figure out the "secret" of creating wealth in network marketing.

- you doubt those who tell you the secret is to keep it simple and not quit.

- exhaustion nips at your enthusiasm.

- fear tempts you to avoid discomfort even if it costs you your future.

- naysayers erode your confidence in the company, compensation or yourself.

- reps or prospects not showing up for meetings makes you want to quit showing up too.

There will be times when others' indifference could make you feel indifferent. There will be times when the unwillingness of others to even consider involvement in your company will make you reconsider your own involvement. Their cynicism will make you cautious. And there will be times when those who have no dreams, no passion, no determination to change their *sitzen leben,* no passion for the thrill of growing a business, will appear wise and relaxed for their choice.

The antidote for these normal experiences and emotions is association. Being with others who remain clearheaded, highly motivated, and full of vitality can quickly infuse and revitalize anyone. Positive association is like a blood transfusion. It is cleansing and renewing. But, unlike a blood transfusion, association in network marketing is also a lot of fun.

Association is the reason those who are serious about growing their businesses will gladly drive long distances to hear the leaders in their company teach. It is why they make time to attend the annual conventions and regional conferences hosted by their company. It is why they clear their schedules to learn from the leaders who have gone before them. They are eager to let the vision, skill, and motivation of other successful individuals rub off on them. Instinctively, they understand the importance of association. They know that "he who walks with wise men (and women) becomes wise."

What are some practical things that reps can do to "keep their heads in the game" through the power of association? In this era, when the world has become a village, it has never been easier. No matter where reps live, there are multiple ways for them to stay connected, focused, and involved. As you look at the following list, ask yourself which of these you and your team are utilizing and which ones you need to take better advantage of:

- weekly group meeting
- weekly in-home meeting
- books
- tape
- video
- telephone

- video-conference
- fax
- voice mail
- e-mail
- conference
- teleconference

Too Busy for Association?

Before my involvement with network marketing, it was unthinkable for me to commit one night a week to anything. I was fiercely protective of my evenings. I could not imagine anything that I could give that kind of time or commitment to. I soon noticed that I did not look at time given to this business as a chore that I resisted. For example, I found myself looking forward to the weekly meetings. They did not detract from my life; they enhanced it.

What was causing such a complete reversal in my thinking? I recognized that several things were happening simultaneously during the time I spent with people in network marketing. I was enjoying being around the most positive, forward-thinking people I had known in years. The more serious they were about their businesses, the more excited they were about where their lives were going. I was learning new things about the industry, my company, and how network marketing works. I was making new friends and meeting new people, and these people impressed me. They were different; their confidence was high; their optimism unmistakable; their friendliness contagious, and their helpfulness unprecedented. They were not afraid of hard work; they had passion for life, and they were willing to do whatever it took to make their dreams become reality.

Association with people of this caliber is good for the soul. It helps us do one very important thing: focus. It encourages us to keep our heads in the game. Sometimes we need others to help us achieve and do what we want. We need others to keep us sharp because in the business of daily life, it is easy to loose the cutting edge.

Executive Coaches: Find One in Your Business

Have you noticed how it has become popular for people to have their own personal physical fitness trainers? Personal trainers are not needed because people need more knowledge about exercise physiology; they are needed to make trainees sweat, stay focused, ignore discomfort, work harder than they have ever worked, and push beyond their old limits of strength. They are needed to help people do what they would not do on their own.

This same phenomenon is occurring in the corporate world. People are hiring individuals like me as executive coaches and corporate trainers. Why do they need us? It is not because we teach them an endless array of concepts that are unique and novel. No! Usually, we tell them what they already know, remind them of what they already want to do, and then help them structure their own life goals and values. When coached over a period of time (usually two or three years), individuals regularly see their productivity go up and their income double and triple. While achieving their goals, these executives have more balance and free time in their lives than ever before. Instead of working more and enjoying it less, they are working less and enjoying it more.

How and why does this happen? Because executive coaches assist individuals in staying on-task. We help them combat one of the fatal flaws of human nature: the desire to do only what seems easiest at the moment. All of us know what it is to take the path of least resistance...to our own demise.

> "Association with others can inspire us to new levels of personal vision and determination."

There are tens of thousands of men and women of character in network marketing who are caring and trust-worthy, people of vision who have learned to say "yes" to their dreams and "no" to distractions. They have the ability to see the future so clearly that it gives them joy and strength in the present. These individuals are our peers and colleagues, and they can serve as a type of executive coach. They remind us of our vision, goals, and desires to grow this business...even when it isn't convenient or easy. Their drive keeps us going. Their tenacity inspires us. Their unwillingness to quit keeps us on the job. Like the army, these people can help us be all that we can be.

Before looking at the last ingredient for success, let me ask you to stop and think about something with me. In counseling, an astute clinician learns to pay attention to the emotions which fill the room. You don't just listen to the content. You listen to the moods, emotions, and atmosphere present in the room. (It may be fear, anxiety, anger, unforgiveness, sadness, stress, joy, peace, happiness, or excitement.)

Have you ever noticed that some people, when they walk into a room, emanate joy while others eliminate it? Some invite laughter, while others eradicate it. Some make you eager to stay, and others make you want to leave. My question to you is this: With what emotion do you fill a room? How do you impact the atmosphere or mood of the places you go? The reason that these questions are worth pondering is that you will do this same thing in your business. And people will intuitively sense what you are filling the room with. Make sure the excitement and joy of growing your business are reflected in your attitude.

INGREDIENT #4: HAVE A PLAN THAT WORKS AND WORK YOUR PLAN

You will hear more and more about it. It will increasingly become the topic *du jour*. Like our presidential elections, you will be weary of hearing about it before it's over. What am I talking about? The increasingly hot topic will be, "How are you going to spend New Year's Eve 1999?" People are going to spend inordinate amounts of time planning, anticipating, and talking about how they intend to usher in the new millennium. They will spend money they don't have in order to party for an evening that will fly by them like a nanosecond. But, in the meantime, it will give them the sensation of inaugurating the new year, decade, century, and millennium in grand style.

In the end, many will realize that they spent years planning for one night. They would have been better off spending one night planning for the next several years. I don't care about the quality of that night. But I do care about the quality of my life in the year 2000. Those who understand this fourth ingredient for success will find themselves wonderfully prepared for both the evening and the era. That is a great place to be. How do we ensure that it happens? It is simpler than many expect.

Look again at the fourth ingredient for success: "Have a plan that works. Work your plan." Two brief sentences. Properly understood, they can change endless numbers of lives. That is because achievement, productivity, accomplishment of significant goals, and success are much less difficult than is normally assumed.

Have a Plan That Works

My objective is not to tell you *which* plan to use for growing your business. I respect whatever plan you and your team are using. There are many differing, but equally effective ways of growing a large team and creating wealth in network marketing. The issue is not "which plan are you using?" but "do you have any plan at all?"

There is no shortage of plans in the corporate world. They abound: old, new, revised, revamped, high tech, low tech, high touch, low touch, simple, complicated, clear, convoluted, elaborate, brief, and on and on. In some cases, they are helpful; sometimes they are hurtful; occasionally, they are laughable, and often they are all but ignored. Countless dollars and human hours go into the business world's endless pursuit of an effective plan. The goal, of course, is to increase revenues. But first, corporate leaders understand they must engender focus and follow-through in their people. They are attempting to increase productivity.

Why is this simple goal so elusive? Because it is completely dependent upon one of the most fascinating dimensions of human behavior: motivation. The dynamics of motivation will be explored from a psychological viewpoint in the remainder of this book. For now, let me take off my clinical hat and write as a business person who is straight-forward and honest. Let me inject a little reality about what is required to succeed in your network marketing business. On the surface, it is ridiculously simple.

Tell It Like It Is

Kenny Troutt has become recognized as one of America's premier corporate leaders. (Not just in the network marketing arena, but in the corporate world as a whole.) When he speaks to groups, he often mentions three qualities he believes are necessary if individuals are to succeed in network marketing. He states:

1. You need a big dream.

2. You must be willing to work hard.

3. You must be willing to see the job through.

I appreciate his candor. He is absolutely correct. It is the third quality which makes success inevitable for some and so elusive for others. But what does this mean, and how do we do it?

There is a common linear progression for people with big dreams. It frequently looks like this:

1. Have a dream.

2. Break the dream down to its component parts or phases.

3. Set goals that reflect the component parts or phases.

4. Develop a plan (long-term, intermediate, and short term) for achievement of each goal.

5. Make your schedule reflect your plan.

6. Stick to your schedule.

If you suddenly feel your eyes glaze over, there is good news. This is not complicated. You already do it all the time. The progression listed above, as Stephen Covey reminds us, is simply "beginning with the end in mind"

> **"Success in network marketing is not about talent. It is about tenacity and steady plodding"**

and then thinking backward from there. It is nothing more than ascertaining *where* you want to go, *how* you are going to get there, and then DOING it.

This process is so automatic that you have already done it numerous times in your own life. You use it for little tasks and for major life goals. You can even do it unconsciously. Have you ever had a large dinner party that left your kitchen in major disarray? When the guests left, you looked around and thought "What a mess!" What did you do next? You began with the end in mind. You set a goal to clean up the kitchen. (I can't bring myself to call cleaning the kitchen a dream...so we will just skip that! But the process is the same.) You began to use some type of plan to organize your goal of a clean kitchen into component parts or phases. Maybe you began by bringing everything into the kitchen and then putting all the food away. Then you threw away all the disposable items. From there, perhaps you stacked the dishes, piled the silverware, gathered the glasses, rinsed these things off, and put them into the dishwasher. You already understood all the necessary steps for the completion of your goal.

Similarly, do you remember when you went to high school or college? What was your dream (your goal)? In the most basic terms, it was to graduate so you could move on to the next goal in your life. You began with the end in mind. As you were entering, you were already planning your exit. How did you do this? You probably met with guidance counselors who helped you move through the six steps above. They respected your goal and then helped you achieve it one year, one semester, one class, one test at a time. In the end, you reached your goal by taking one step at a time.

Stairway to Success

Every good network marketing company has a clearly defined "stairway to success." It is a graph or narrative description that allows participants to understand where they enter the business and what is required to work their way up the ranks of increasing leadership and revenue. One company actually calls its hierarchy of progressive leadership and revenues the "stairway to success." It is a great phrase.

The word "stairs" is a great metaphor for growth in business as well as in life. Imagine going to visit friends in a third-floor office. After climbing the stairs, you find the office and then you knock on the door. What would happen if, when your friends saw you standing there, they began to admire, applaud, and praise you for reaching the third-floor office? What if everyone went on and on,

shook your hand, patted you on the back, and congratu-
lated you as if you had just run a marathon? You'd start
thinking these people were up to something besides work.
Why? Because climbing a set of steps is not a noteworthy
achievement. It's no big deal. You did it without even
thinking. But you DID do something amazing. You just
made a vertical climb of about 40 feet above ground level.
It seemed inconsequential because all you did was take
one step at a time, and before you knew it, you were at
your destination. This is precisely how success is achieved
in the growth of a business...one step at a time.

So if you are one of those people who do not like to
dream big, see too far into the future, or come up with
elaborate ways to plan and manage your future, that is
okay. Just see which step you are standing on now in your
business, then do what it takes to go up to the next one.
It is okay to keep your goals small and your progress
steady.

People who get to the top through systematic planning and action often seem to think they got there almost by accident. They are perplexed because others
marvel at their success. To their way of thinking, they
did not do anything spectacular. They just took one step
at a time and refused to quit. This is why success in network marketing (and most of life) is not about talent. It
is about tenacity and steady plodding.*

If success is easier than most people anticipate, then
why do so few achieve it? Whether it is succeeding in network marketing or any other business endeavor, why do
some people not succeed? Apart from not knowing and
applying the three principles of network marketing and
the four ingredients for success, there is one other important principle that is helpful for them to grasp. It is the
art of learning to live in a new time zone. The time zone of
entrepreneurial time. So look at your watch; wind your
clock. The next chapter is all about this new kind of time.

* (If you want to see a good comedy that drives home the point of taking one step at a time, rent the movie *What About Bob?* It is a great story about "Bob," played by the inimitable Bill Murray, who conquers fears by taking "baby steps.")

CHAPTER FOUR

LIVING IN ENTREPRENEURIAL TIME

You may have heard the story about the two groups of people in the universe. In this story, each group lives on a separate planet. One group of people lives on "planet normal." On the other planet are those individuals involved in network marketing.

The vast majority of people in this universe live on planet normal, where it is customary for most of the inhabitants to be employed by someone else. It is an accepted cultural norm that these people are told by their employers what tasks they can perform, where they will work, and when they will work. Curiously, on planet normal, most of the people do not work because they are pursuing a dream. They work only to receive a paycheck every week or two. Additionally, they allow their employers to determine the monetary value of their work. While the inhabitants of this planet regularly wish they were receiving more revenue, they rarely seriously consider acting on any creative alternatives. They are so thoroughly acculturated to this way of life that anything different from what they know is viewed as an alternative, abnormal life style.

Meanwhile, on the second planet in this universe, are those individuals involved in network marketing. On this planet people are driven by different values. They are not willing to endlessly trade their limited amount of time for a fixed amount of dollars. They are motivated by a desire for freedom. Freedom to pursue their own dreams. Freedom to test the limits of their skills. Freedom of time. Freedom to be paid what they are worth. And freedom from financial constraint. These people know that those on planet normal view them as if they were half crazy. Similarly, when they look at the inhabitants of planet normal, they cannot comprehend how those people willingly yield such important areas of life over to others. Indeed, these two groups are worlds apart.

What does this story portray? It represents two completely different views about the world we live in. One is a world full of daring proactive people who see opportunity and choose to hold the reins of their futures in their own hands. The other is a place where individuals are more risk averse, prefer to keep life safe and predictable, and give their dreams and the reins of their lives over to others. In short, this story is a wonderful illustration of life as an entrepreneur and as a nonentrepreneur.

Two Types of Entrepreneurs: Primary or Macroentrepreneurs and Microentrepreneurs

I classify entrepreneurs into two categories: primary or macroentrepreneurs and microentrepreneurs. People like Bill Gates and Kenny Troutt are primary entrepreneurs. They are pure entrepreneurs. In their minds, they see the world at the macro level. As primary entrepreneurs, they view the world like an astronaut in space peering out through a porthole. To them the world looks small, reachable, and manageable.

Microentrepreneurs are also people of exceptional vision, although their vision is not as expansive and bold as that of a primary entrepreneur. They may not see the world at a glance, but they nonetheless have a keen eye for discerning business or financial potential. They also have the heart of an entrepreneur within them. Within this heart lies a mixture of courage, a willingness to take some risk, and a quiet but relentless desire to be their best.

The beauty of network marketing is that it provides entrepreneurs an environment wherein their courage and vision can be merged with those of macroentrepreneurs. When these entrepreneurs select a reputable company, their vision will effortlessly fit into the wake that follows every primary or macroentrepreneur who is charting new courses.

Whether macro or micro, what does it mean to be an entrepreneur? Do entrepreneurs see, think, and work in ways that are different from those who are not entrepreneurs? And what has this got to do with success in network marketing?

Life in a New Time Zone: Entrepreneurial Time Versus Bureaucratic Time

Have you ever had several meetings on the same day in three different time zones? Your body clock might be in one time zone; your wrist watch indicates a second time zone, and the clock on the meeting room wall indicates a third. It can get a little wild trying to keep track of what time zone you are in. Life in network marketing is just like this. If we don't pay close attention, we can become totally confused about where we are, what time zone we are in, and how to live in that time zone.

Dan Sullivan is an excellent executive coach from Toronto, Canada. He breaks life in the business world into two categories: Entrepreneurial Time and Bureaucratic Time. His categories are wonderfully applicable to growing a network marketing business. When people in network marketing learn the vast difference between these two time zones and learn to pay attention to which zone they are living or thinking in, then growing their businesses becomes much more understandable and fun.

Life in Bureaucratic Time

What is the difference between entrepreneurial time and bureaucratic time? As Dan Sullivan makes clear, people who live in bureaucratic time live in a much more structured and predictable world. For example, people living in bureaucratic time generally know how many hours they will work each day and week. They know how much they will earn per hour. They can give you accurate estimates of what they will earn each week, month, and year. They know the number of sick days, health days, and vacation days they have coming to them. Their lives have a routine and a rhythm with which they are well acquainted. Those who live in entrepreneurial time pay little attention to these things, as the rest of this chapter will make clear. Their thoughts and focus are on much more important things.

When Bureaucratic Beliefs Meet Entrepreneurial Time

In network marketing, countless individuals start their network marketing businesses wanting to be entrepreneurs who live in entrepreneurial time. Inadvertently, they end up living in bureaucratic time. They forget which time zone they need to think and live in. When this happens, it is easy to become disoriented.

For example, some people take expectations from the world of bureaucratic time (or "planet normal") and try to apply them in the world of entrepreneurial time. It will not work. There is little successful interface between the two. The most common concept people bring from the bureaucratic time zone and attempt to force-fit into the entrepreneurial time zone is that of "linear income".

> "Entrepreneurs can see things sooner, more clearly, and more fully than others."

Those who live in bureaucratic time are accustomed to seeing a direct correlation between the hours they have worked and the compensation they have received. If they work for five hours they expect to get paid for five hours. If they work for a month they expect to get paid for a month's work. This is the norm in a bureaucratic time zone. It is standard fare. But when this expectation or belief is transferred into entrepreneurial time, it is death. These people unconsciously begin to think, "I have been in this business for three months, and I have not seen a paycheck commensurate with three months of work. Something is wrong here! Somebody pay me something for my work."

Their old beliefs from another time zone confuse and frustrate them when they don't transfer into entrepreneurial time. But some reps have lived with these beliefs for so long that they don't question the applicability in their businesses or in entrepreneurial time. Instead, they will question whether their network marketing businesses can really work for them. In reality, they can work just fine for them, but not until they learn and accept a new way of measuring time and changing expectations.

I recently heard a primary entrepreneur speak to reps in his company. He kiddingly stated, "Where else can you work one hundred hours and get paid nothing? And then you can work five hours and get paid for one thousand hours?" What is he talking about? He understands life in entrepreneurial time. He knows that in entrepreneurial time you do not expect or look for any correlation between how hard or how long you worked and the income received! On the front end you work very hard and expect next to nothing in return. And on the back end you are paid far more than you worked for. This is life in a new time zone. It is why we teach people to take a long-term approach to the growth of their businesses. It takes time to grow our organizations. It takes time to create depth and ongoing duplication. It takes time to develop a team and create serious residual income. Those who can develop and maintain a mindset of living in entrepreneurial time understand this. Those who slip back into bureaucratic time grow impatient and confused.

HOW ENTREPRENEURS THINK

How do entrepreneurs think? Let's take a typical entrepreneur named Joe. If you could get into his mind, see with his eyes, and walk around in his body for several days, what would you discover? You would quickly sense that an entrepreneur thinks and works very differently from those who live in bureaucratic time. The first thing you would discover is that they have extraordinary vision.

Entrepreneurs Have 2/2000 Vision

Look at the chart below. It represents how ophthalmologists and optometrists tell us about the quality of our eyesight.

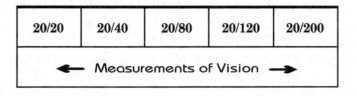

20/20	20/40	20/80	20/120	20/200
← Measurements of Vision →				

The number on the left side of the hash mark represents what you can see clearly at a distance of twenty feet. The number on the right represents a standardized norm. In other words, it tells us where people with good eyesight can stand to see the same object with the same clarity that the person being tested can see at twenty feet. So, if someone has 20/40 vision, this means that they can see at twenty feet what people with good eyesight can see at forty feet away. If someone has 20/120 vision, it suggests that what they see clearly at twenty feet others see clearly at one hundred and twenty feet away.

What has this got to do with how entrepreneurs think and see the world? It represents what exceptional vision entrepreneurs have. They see potential, opportunity, trends, transitions, emerging markets, needs, and the future with an acuity that leaves nonentrepreneurs feeling myopic or blind. This is because entrepreneurs can see things sooner, more clearly, and more fully than others. Look at the graph below.

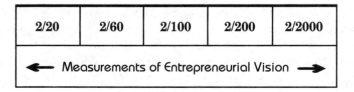

2/20	2/60	2/100	2/200	2/2000
← Measurements of Entrepreneurial Vision →				

In this graph the number on the left represents what the average person can see at a distance of two feet away. The number on the right represents the varying degrees of vision of different entrepreneurs. For example, 2/20 means that the average person can see at a distance of two feet what an entrepreneur can see clearly at twenty feet; 2/100 suggests that what is visible to the normal population at two feet is effortlessly clear to a second entrepreneur at one hundred feet. And for some, 2/2000 represents entrepreneurial eyesight like an eagle. These entrepreneurs can see with perfect clarity at two thousand feet what others cannot see at two feet.

Primary entrepreneurs have vision that is genuinely astonishing. Not only can they see things long before we can see them, they can see things that we cannot see at all! No matter how much they try to explain to us what they see with perfect clarity, we sometimes cannot see it at all. In fact, we cannot even imagine what they are talking about, let alone clearly see what they themselves see!

Showing Your Business Presentation to Someone Is Like Giving a Vision Test

I have chosen a base line of two feet for measuring entrepreneurial vision. That is because when reps show their businesses to others, the prospect is usually about two feet away from the materials used as a visual aid to present their businesses. What reps are doing, whether they know it or not, is giving people a vision test. They are trying to ascertain if the prospect has any entrepreneurial vision.

You may have shown your business presentation to someone, and they just looked at you with an expression that says, "I have not got the foggiest idea what you are talking about!" Their facial expression is telling you the truth. They literally do not see what you are showing them. It is right in front of their eyes but they cannot grasp it.

Next time this happens to you, don't take it personally. Just smile and be thankful that you have good eyesight. You see what others don't. Additionally, the more entrenched someone is in the world of bureaucratic time, the less likely they are to get involved or excited about what you are doing and offering to them. They don't get it. Be gracious, move on, and look for someone with better eyesight.

Entrepreneurs Can See Around Corners

Another way to appreciate the vision of entrepreneurs is to recognize that they have the ability to see the future, or, to "see around corners." If you were sitting in a room with someone, you would generally expect to see whatever they see. But what would it be like if you were sitting in a room with someone who had the same visual field as you but they could see much more? What if they could look beyond the closed door, down the hall, around the corner, and down two flights of stairs to see your best friend approaching? If they announced to you that your best friend was on the way to see you and then two minutes later that friend walked into the room, you would be astonished. This is precisely what entrepreneurs are able to do. They see the future approaching in ways that leave others feeling visually impaired.

The next time you have the oppportunity to listen to macroentrepreneurs, pay careful attention. Listen to them when they describe the future of their industries, companies, and products or services. Listen to them, but stop paying attention to the information they are sharing. Instead, pay attention to them as people - primary entrepreneurs. They are attempting to let you into their minds so that you can see the world with their eyes. They are describing to you an approaching reality. They are looking into the future and around corners. They can *literally see in their imaginations what they are describing with words.*

I admire all primary entrepreneurs for their skills. But I have spent enough time with numerous entrepreneurs over the years so that I admire them even more for something else. True visionaries and pure entrepreneurs live with a unique loneliness while they wait for others to finally begin to see or grasp what they have seen for years. Oswald Sanders wrote about leaders with exceptional vision, "There is no one more lonely than a man ahead of his time." Leaders with vision see things first. They see further into the future. And they see things more fully and clearly than the people around them. That can be a lonely place. And it is a difficult balancing act to keep pursuing your vision at high speed while going slow enough for the people who are trying to keep up.

On a much smaller scale, this is the same experience many participants in network marketing have. They have wonderful vision, and they can see potential and opportunity in their businesses. But when they begin to share "what they see" with other people, they soon realize that most others cannot see what they see. In these moments the rep can stay strong and be thankful for particularly good eyesight, or can be tempted to feel the loneliness of foresight and get discouraged.

You Can Improve Your Entrepreneurial Vision

Our capacity to think and see the world as an entrepreneur is not fixed. It can develop and grow. That is why association with other visionaries is so vital. They can impact our thinking and enhance our vision. In contradistinction to this, naysayers will pluck your eyes out if you let them.

Paul Orberson, like countless others, is a great example of someone whose entrepreneurial vision has improved with time. How far could Paul Orberson see when he got involved with his network marketing company?

His goal was to make enough money to pay for a new pick-up truck! That means that on a good day, the farthest Paul could see into the future was to generate about $350 bucks per month. Since he currently earns more than $1 million per month, I would guess his vision has improved. I think he can see things now that heretofore he could not even imagine.

> *"The most surprising aspect of success is how deceptively simple it is."*

How far do you think most new participants in a network marketing company can see? On their best days, many of them can barely see past recouping their initial investments. That is why when we show this business to people, there is little point in telling them how big the opportunity really is. It is so far beyond what they can imagine, see, or comprehend that it is counterproductive to even mention it to them. Simply listen for their dreams, desires, or discontentedness and share how your company might be the vehicle to get them where they want to go in life.

Entrepreneurs Live in a Resource State

You have heard the expression, "It's all a state of mind." There is truth to this.

Our state of mind has a profound impact on our view of life and the world. Let's look at two specific categories.

A resource state and a problem state. Successful entrepreneurs learn to live in a resource state.

RESOURCE STATE	PROBLEM STATE
• anticipates the future with confidence.	• anticipates the future with dread.
• views problems as something that can and will be solved.	• views problems as something that will not be solved.
• believes life is good while knowing it can also be difficult.	• believes life is hard and good moments are the exception.
• sees challenges as things that can be managed and overcome.	• sees challenges as unmanageable and overwhelming.
• sees possibilities everywhere.	• sees problems everywhere.
• enjoys life	• endures life.
• expects to thrive and win in the game of life.	• expects to just survive in the game of life.
• feels like a player in the game of life.	• feels like a victim in the game of life.

ENTREPRENEURS LIVE WITH AN OVER-ALL ATTITUDE OF POSITIVE EXPECTANCY

People who live in a resource state, or a state of excellence, know they have some measure of control over their environments and their futures. They know they are players in the game of life. They see the future with such clarity and confidence that they are not overwhelmed by their immediate circumstances.

You Can LEARN to Live in a Resource State

It is possible to watch reps grow in their abilities to consistently remain in a resource state. As their convictions about the industry of network marketing grows, along with their confidence in their company and its compensation potential, so does their poise and confidence. They become unshakable. As the big picture gets clearer to them, the normal problems of growing any business become less problematic. These reps become more resilient, tougher, and more optimistic. They know that their future successes do not hang on the response of one person or one appointment. Getting to this level of internal confidence takes time. But it is very freeing. To other people this freedom can at times be misinterpreted as "an attitude."

I can look as if I have "an attitude" to people. If they don't understand my confidence in network marketing and the company I have affiliated with, then they could mistake my confidence for indifference or arrogance. I regularly share a common story with people who are considering joining my team but cannot decide. They are vacillating between yes, no, and maybe. I usually say something like this:

Let me share a story with you that might take the pressure off of you. Do you know that every single week night at 6:30 and 9:30 a British Airways jet leaves Dulles International Airport for London? Do you know what intrigues me about these flights? They are going with or without us. It doesn't matter if we are on them.

Just like those British Airways flights, the industry of network marketing is going to take off and become a trillion dollar industry, with or without us. It doesn't matter if we are there.

And my company is going to take off and become a multibillion dollar company, with or without us. It doesn't matter if we are there.

I am going to take advantage of this opportunity with or without you. I purchased a ticket for this flight. I want to know, do you want to fly with us? Do you see how my company can be a vehicle to make your dreams a reality, and do you want to join my team? I would love to have you. But it really doesn't matter to me what you decide. Your future may hang on your decision. But mine doesn't. So what do you want to do?

This may seem blunt to you as a reader. But when you say this to people they actually appreciate your candor and feel less pressure. They intuitively know that you are in a resource state and that their response is not going to send you into a problem state. It allows them to be as honest with you as you have been with them. It is freeing for everyone.

Reps Living in Entrepreneurial Time Are Very Special People

When reps learn to live in entrepreneurial time, improve their vision, and live in a resource state, they are much less flappable. Standard parts of the business, such as being stood up for appointments or "no shows" for meetings, are much less bothersome. Why? Because the future is seen with such clarity and inevitability that the routine aspects of the business are accepted as inconsequential. They know with certainty that the future of the industry, their selected company, and their compensation does not hang on any one appointment...no matter who it is with. So like a Judo expert, they just roll with it and keep going. (Jimmy Dick, a true industry expert and someone enroute to making $1 million per month in his business, has his own expression for these situations. He quips that successful reps develop a "rubber butt." No matter what happens, they just bounce right back up and keep going.)

Entrepreneurs who live in a resource state also begin to realize what a small percentage of the population they represent. So when the majority of people do not see what they see, or have a willingness to do what they will do, entrepreneurs are not surprised, and they don't take it personally. They know they are looking for select people who make up a small portion of the population. Look at the triangle below and imagine it as a filter that the entire population is run through.

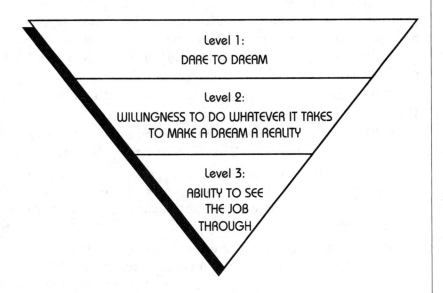

Level 1:
DARE TO DREAM

Level 2:
WILLINGNESS TO DO WHATEVER IT TAKES
TO MAKE A DREAM A REALITY

Level 3:
ABILITY TO SEE
THE JOB
THROUGH

What percentage of the population do you think really has a clear dream? Now, of those people who have a dream, how many do you believe are willing to do whatever it takes to make their dreams become a reality? Of those who have made it through the first two levels of our filter, how many do you think have the willingness "to see the job through?" By the time you get through the third stage of our filtering process, you realize that we are looking for a small fraction of the population. Or, as Pat Hintze, a man who epitomizes all that is honorable about this industry says, network marketing "is just difficult enough to weed out those who don't really want it."

Understanding this filtering process is very liberating. It keeps people in a resource state. Their focus shifts from those people who decline an invitation to change their lives, and it shifts to envisioning what it will be like, one day, to have on their team thirty other motivated people who do have a dream, the willingness to work hard, and the ability to see the job through. In their resource state they see the future with such positive expectancy that they barely notice those who choose not to get involved. Where are you? Do you dwell on those who have, or will, say "yes" to your invitation? Or do you dwell on those who say "no"?

This filtering process suggests several fascinating things:

- The people who persist in network marketing are very special people. They deserve to be honored.

- The number of people willing to go through all three stages of the filtering process is so small we never have to worry about market saturation in our industry.

- If you have gone to the effort to purchase this book and read this far, you are a very special person yourself. The heart of an entrepreneur is beating inside of you. Protect it, and keep it healthy.

HOW ENTREPRENEURS WORK

They Talk Themselves Into Staying On-Task

Talk to any of the top income earners in network marketing. You will quickly discover they all have the entrepreneurial work ethic. They talk themselves *into* staying on-task while others talk themselves *out* of staying on-task. They regularly do the little things in the business, and that makes all the difference. They may not like to pick up the phone and call a prospect or do a follow-up call, but they will do it anyway. They don't let their momentary discomfort derail them from pursuing their dreams. They see and know what they want in their future and do what they can today to make it happen.

> "...not only does the dream have to come from within, so does the desire, discipline, and drive."

Entrepreneurs have the same internal battle with themselves that others have. They just win more of the battles. When contacting people, they also wrestle with occasional doubt, fear, and fatigue. They don't enjoy being misunderstood by others. Their thoughts and feelings are just like anyone else's at the critical moments of decision. They debate with themselves about calling someone "right now" instead of tomorrow. What is special about entrepreneurs is their reactions to these common struggles. They don't yield to their immediate feelings or thoughts at the expense of their life goals and dreams. They focus on where they are going and what they want out of life, and they subjugate their desires to avoid any anxiety they might feel to their drive to achieve a dream.

Listen to the strategy for staying on-task from an individual who has never felt comfortable calling people on the phone. When her mental battle begins, and fear tempts her to postpone making the call, she asks herself, "If someone were going to pay me five hundred dollars to make this one-minute call, would I do it? And if I could be paid for years to come for making this brief call, would I do it?" Her questions prompt her to remember the big picture, stay on-task, and push through her temporary dislike of phoning people. No wonder she is a major player in her company.

They Become Their Own Worst Boss

David Jennings is one of the highest income earners in his network marketing company. When teaching people about his business, he regularly speaks of "being the worst boss you ever had." What does he mean? Don't people get into this business precisely because they don't want a boss, quotas, or someone telling them what to do? Absolutely. But David recognizes that the best thing about network marketing can also be the worst thing. Some people, when they have no one telling them what to do, end up getting nothing done! In network marketing, not only does the dream have to come from within, so does the desire, discipline, and drive. A wise boss will help people be productive and successful.

In the ordinary work world some people dream of an easygoing boss. In the world of network marketing and in entrepreneurial time, an easygoing boss will cost you your dream.

My suggestion is to be tough with yourself and patient with others. Recognize that in network marketing you have what you wanted: Your future is in your hands. But, while accepting responsibility for growing your business, give grace to other reps. Their dreams may still be developing, their vision growing, and their confidence emerging. Cut them some slack while giving yourself no room for excuses.

Entrepreneurs Understand the Need for Association With a Positive Reference Group

While working, entrepreneurs regularly make time to associate with peers who understand their world. Why do they do this? Because they understand the value of this time. They know time with a positive reference group will:

- *keep them on the cutting edge of knowledge*
- *keep them on the cutting edge of enthusiasm*
- *keep them on the cutting edge of conviction*
- *keep them focused, accountable, and on-task*

They do whatever it takes to remain in a state of excellence. And time with other positive, motivated, like-minded people is a high priority for them. Compare those reps you know who are plugged into weekly meetings, who attend conferences, and who use a voice mail system to those who are lone rangers. You quickly see why entrepreneurs look for positive reference groups.

They All Wear Nikes

Entrepreneurs keep their dreams in mind at the macro level but they remain exceptionally balanced in their daily lives. They see what needs to be done and then follow the Nike philosophy. They "just do it." Whether they need to pick up the phone, send a fax, mail something, or do any other task, they distinguish themselves by this one quality. They simply do what needs to be done. They produce instead of procrastinate. This quality, above many others, is what determines who is a winner and who is a "wannabe."

They grasp the wisdom of Alcoholics Anonymous which suggests that people "do the next right thing." This has a way of keeping life remarkably simple, focused, and steadily progressing toward the realization of dreams.

When you meet entrepreneurs who have consistently stayed on-task, they are remarkably calm about their achievements and successes. Why? Because to them success was just a journey which began with an idea they pursued *one step at a time*. Those of us viewing their accomplishments from a distance see what they did as one single event, as if they reached their goal in one superhuman vertical leap. But to them it was accomplished one task, one moment, one day at a time. They know that success is simply a function of relentless effort and qual-

> *"Entrepreneurs follow the Nike philosophy. They "just do it."*

ity time. They agree with Woody Allen: "Eighty percent of life is just showing up!" But we honor them, because, like Cal Ripken, they kept showing up - no matter what. They put on their Nikes, stayed on-task, and did the next right thing.

Recently, I called a friend to see how his day at the office went. As president of his company, he had spearheaded a bid on a project and faced fierce competition. The bid proposal had taken ten years to develop and cost $17 million. It was a $7 billion-project, winner take all. I knew that the bid winner's name was being announced that day. In my mind this was anything but a normal day at the office for my friend! I asked him how it went, and he told me that his company had won. They had been awarded the $7 billion contract.

The next part of our conversation was the most revealing. I asked him what he and his staff did and how they celebrated after the announcement. (I wondered if they might all take the rest of the afternoon off, have a party, or go out to dinner.) He said, "We opened a bottle of champagne, had a toast, and then we all went back to work." How could these people be so successful and yet so casual? To them this was not the celebration of a record-breaking vertical leap. It was the culminating moment of a ten year journey full of countless small steps. And taking each step, one at a time, was simply a way of life for these diligent people.

There is a very surprising aspect to success. It is not how elusive and difficult it is. It is not how it can only be visited upon a few fortunate individuals. On the contrary, *the most surprising aspect of success is how deceptively simple it is*. Set your goals, do the next right thing, and don't quit.

The idea of being an entrepreneur is new to many people. They may have had a fleeting desire to be one but they never took the idea seriously. Don't dismiss this idea. If you do, you are dismissing yourself. Embrace the idea of learning to think and live as an entrepreneur. Give yourself permission to learn how to live in entrepreneurial time. Associate with people whose vision will improve your own. Practice living in a resource state, and put on your Nikes. It will change your life.

CHAPTER FIVE

REALITY CHECK FOR FINANCIAL EXPECTATIONS

Network marketing. The longer I am in this world of the future the more passionate I am about it. There is, however, one dimension about life in the world of network marketing that stands out. In fact, I find it amazing: The unrealistic monetary expectations of some people who get involved with it. For some of these reps there is little correlation between their expectations and reality. They have minimal awareness of what it takes to make a dream become reality and what it takes to *grow* a business—any business.

Some people in network marketing seem to think financial success should be effortlessly within reach. To them, success is like trying to get something off of the top shelf of a closet. All that is necessary is to briefly stand on your tiptoes, stretch your arms as far as possible, and then feel your hand on the prize. In network marketing, and any other goal in life that is significant, the ability to grasp with our hands what we see with our eyes in the distance requires a long, steady walk.

There are numerous network marketing companies which can be very lucrative; there are millions of dollars to be made. The potential is real; true wealth is attainable. It can be attained quickly, relative to the traditional methods utilized to create wealth. But the big departure from reality occurs in what some people think is required to create this wealth. This potential becomes reality only for those who remain focused, tenacious, and undeterred in the pursuit of their goals.

Let's do a reality check and have some fun looking at this. In the Jeff Foxworthy school of "you know you are a redneck if...." let's take a quiz. We'll call ours:

YOU KNOW YOUR FINANCIAL EXPECTATIONS ARE IN NEED OF ADJUSTMENT IF:

- You thought you could create wealth without hard work.

- You thought you could work this business on a part-time basis but immediately receive a full-time income.

- You thought the top income earners in network marketing became wealthy because of luck and good timing and not because of hard work.

- You thought you could grow your network marketing business, become wealthy, and never experience any disappointment.

- You thought most of your family and friends would immediately join you in your endeavor.

- You thought simple was the same thing as easy.

- You believed most Americans have a dream, and they are just waiting for the right vehicle to make their dream a reality.

- You thought there would be no learning curve in this business.

- You expected every rep you sponsored to be a self-starter and able to sustain his or her own focus.

- You thought you could do this business alone and had no need to plug yourself or your reps into any system.

- You thought you could treat network marketing like a minor hobby but have it pay you like a major business.

- You thought you could work your business sporadically but have it grow steadily.

- You thought you could merely *play* with your business, but it would *work* for you.

- You thought your company founders were giving people money instead of an opportunity.

- You thought you could build this business and never leave your comfort zone.

- You thought you could build your own multimillion-dollar business by only working a few minutes a week.

- You saw serious residual income but forgot that it takes significant time and effort to build an organization that has depth and duplication.

- You thought you could make small investments of effort in your business and reap huge revenues in return.

- You thought you could grow a business and not have to grow as a person.

- You thought "no strain, no pain, no gain" only applied in weight rooms.

- You thought you could have success without sweat.

- You thought you don't need to be tough to triumph.

How did you do on the quiz? Personally, I flunked. At least I did in the early months of building my business. Before getting started in network marketing, I was absolutely thorough in my research of my chosen company and the future of this industry. And I was absolutely naive in my expectations of what it would take to grow my business to the point where it was generating six figures per month. In short, I initially failed to recognize two things:

1. I needed to invest substantial amounts of time and energy in my business if I wanted it to return substantial revenue back to me.

2. The return I expected on my investment was much too small. My dreams, expectations, and goals all needed to be significantly increased. The opportunity to participate in a high-quality

network marketing company is bigger than I initially imagined.

Maybe, like me, you are realizing that growing your business to significant levels of income is tougher and takes more time than you initially expected. Maybe, like me, you did not know that there are three stages of network marketing. And maybe, like me, once you know these three stages, you will be free to settle in, accept reality, and work hard. Investing diligently on the front end of your business can yield an investment return that is literally life-changing on the back end. It is hard work. And it is worth every minute of it ...*in the end.*

THE THREE PSYCHOLOGICAL STAGES OF NETWORK MARKETING

STAGE #1. IT'S NOT WORTH IT
STAGE #2. IT'S WORTH IT
STAGE #3. I'M NOT WORTH THIS MUCH

A friend and I were driving to a meeting and discussing these three psychological stages of growing a network marketing business. (When you are driving over 200 miles to do a business presentation, you have time to discuss a few things.) We started to compare these stages to an old question you have probably heard. "Given the choice, would you rather have a million dollars or a penny that is doubled each day for a month?" It is one of those questions that is so common it loses its impact. We stop paying attention to its meaning. To understand the magnitude of the question we did the math. The numbers reminded us of why we need to take the long view in this business.

A PENNY DOUBLED EACH DAY FOR ONE MONTH

STAGE ONE		STAGE TWO	
The "It's Not Worth It!" Stage		*The "It's Worth It!" Stage*	
DAY 1	$0.01	DAY 20	$5,242.88
DAY 2	$0.02	DAY 21	$10,485.76
DAY 3	$0.04	DAY 22	$20,971.52
DAY 4	$0.08	DAY 23	$41,943.04
DAY 5	$0.16	DAY 24	$83,886.08
DAY 6	$0.32		
DAY 7	$0.64	STAGE THREE	
DAY 8	$1.28	*The "I'm Not Worth*	
DAY 9	$2.56	*This Much!" Stage*	
DAY 10	$5.12		
DAY 11	$10.24	DAY 25	$167,772.16
DAY 12	$20.48	DAY 26	$335,544.32
DAY 13	$40.96	DAY 27	$671,088.64
DAY 14	$81.92	DAY 28	$1,342,177.28
DAY 15	$163.84	DAY 29	$2,684,354.56
DAY 16	$327.68	DAY 30	$5,368,709.12
DAY 17	$655.36	DAY 31	$10,737,418.24
DAY 18	$1,310.72		
DAY 19	$2,621.44		

The Three Psychological Stages of Growing a Network Marketing Business

Look carefully at this chart. It is wonderfully illustrative of what it is like to grow a network marketing business. There are three definite stages that we have to go through. We cannot get to Stage Three without going through Stage Two, and we cannot get to Stage Two without spending time and paying our dues in Stage One. There are no shortcuts. Reps may go through these stages at different speeds but they definitely go through them and not around them. Not one of the top income earners in network marketing was able to bypass these stages. No exceptions.

LIFE IN STAGE ONE

People who are in Stage One and earnestly attempting to grow their businesses will inevitably have moments when they think, "It's not worth it." Look at Day Seven in the chart. Earnings are not yet $1 a day; at Day Fourteen, they are not yet $100. If this were the up-front salary for a rep, you can see why there would be the temptation to quit. And if these days represented weeks or months, instead of days, you can see why it would be even more tempting to quit.

Who would work hard for seventeen months and be satisfied with a return of $655? No one. People don't keep going in Stage One because they are satisfied. They keep going because they have a dream. They are living in entrepreneurial time with vision of 2/100 or 2/1000. They can see around corners. Their association with a positive reference group sustains them while they wait for their hopes to become reality.

A Common Mistake

The most common mistake people make in Stage One is to judge its effectiveness by linear income. They slip back to a bureaucratic time zone. Then, as previously noted, they begin to look for a direct correlation with the amount of time worked and the income received. When they don't see a check commensurate with linear expectations, they

77

check out. The only way to enjoy Stage One and get through it is to keep living in entrepreneurial time. If you're going to sustain your motivation in the present while waiting for the dollars to get serious in the future, you have to understand the power and genius of network marketing.

> *"In network marketing entrepreneurs are paid for their vision, courage, and stamina."*

It is important to understand how the compensation in your particular company works. You must be motivated by realistic goals and then be willing to do what is necessary to achieve the compensation level you desire. There is a vast difference between looking forward to Stages Two and Three of a network marketing business with the vision, mindset, and work ethic of an entrepreneur, versus seeing the same numbers as a distant wish without the will to turn them into an attainable goal.

Some reps enter network marketing as if it were a simple two-step line dance. In Step One, each new participant sends one check to the network marketing company of his or her choice. In Step Two, the selected company sends increasingly larger checks back to the participants each month.

In actuality, network marketing is a three-step dance. The First Step is when participants get started by affiliating with a company. Step Three is when the company begins to send checks back to the participants. Between these two simple steps is another that is more difficult and less appealing. It is called sustained, hard work. Focus. Until this step is accepted, it is difficult to be patient with the growth of business in Stage One.

I have to admit, adjusting to the reality of Stage One was a major transition for me. In my professional career, people seek me out. They initiate, they call, and they pay. I am accustomed to having corporate heads and members of Congress *call me* for individual appointments or for speaking engagements. It has been this way for twenty years. I like it this way. Now to take advantage of this network marketing oppportunity, I have to initiate calling, I have to be the aggressor, and I have to do what is necessary to build a thriving business. It was not a small adjustment, but it was worth making. I know I am not alone. For example, anyone who has gotten through Stage One knows experientially what it is like:

- to fly to another city to do a meeting and find out there are no new guests.
- to work at a regular job and then get in the car and drive 250 miles to be at a meeting where there are no new prospects.
- to have someone arrange to meet for a business presentation meeting or for a meal to discuss the business, and they don't show up. And they may not even call to tell you they will not be present.
- to spend precious time, energy, or money to go to a meeting that is a complete waste of time.
- to sign up a new rep with an abundance of talent who then does nothing.

This is part of the reality of Stage One. And there is no way to avoid it. Does anyone enjoy this dimension of the business? Not if they're normal. So how do they get through it? They usually do two things, even if they are not consciously aware of it: They accept this as an unavoidable aspect of doing this business, and they apply many of the concepts we have been discussing thus far in this book. These two things allow them to stay focused and committed while pursuing Stage Two or Three.

Chasing Fool's Gold

What I find endlessly amusing about people in network marketing is what they do when they get a taste of life in Stage One. As soon as it gets difficult, many of them quit, or they go looking for a "new deal." Those who go looking for the new, better, easier deal are chasing fool's gold. They live with the mythology that they are going to get something for nothing. And there seems to be a never-ending stream of new network marketing "opportunities" which specifically prey on those who have little knowledge of what it takes to grow a business. They get hoodwinked into believing that the "next deal" will allow them to bypass Stage One. Like they are playing Monopoly, they keep waiting for something that says, "go immediately to 'go' and collect $200." It may happen in board games but it rarely happens in the game of life. Network marketing is an invitation to grow a business and tap into the profits of the industry with which your particular company is affiliated. It is neither an invitation to play the lottery nor the equivalent of a hot tip on a horse race.

For those who become involved in network marketing with some naïve expectations like I did, there are two choices. They can adapt, or they can exit. Whatever they decide, the consequence of each choice will be profoundly determinative.

I have made my choice. I am going to Stage Three. But if I had known the things discussed so far in this book, they would have reduced my confusion and increased my resolve in those moments which were less than exhilarating.

Foundational Principles for Success

Let's briefly review some of the foundational principles of growing our businesses. The principles constitute the compass that gives us direction when we are lost in the fog of Stage One.

- The three principles of network marketing are consistent effort, duplication, and "give it enough time." They remind us to work steadily, replicate our efforts, and be patient.
- Mama said there would be days like this. Stop fighting reality. Accept it. Stay on-task.
- This is a marathon, not a sprint. That is why a pack horse is better than a race horse.
- Success in network marketing is more about tenacity than talent. No matter what, don't quit.
- Wealth comes from depth. Depth comes from duplication. Duplication comes from having a system. Keep the system simple. Wealth is not accidental.
- Measure time in the business like a pilot: hours logged. The one who shows the most business presentations wins.
- Stay in a resource state; get out of the problem state. Let the certainty of future success provide joy, vigor, and confidence today.
- Be your own worst boss. Associate with a positive reference group.

You might want to make note of this page in your book. When you or someone you are working with is feeling like this business is "not worth it," the above principles for success will provide a good reality check.

STAGE TWO: IT'S WORTH IT!

Those who grow their businesses consistently and effectively will reach Stage Two. This is the point where reps begin to feel that the financial returns they are receiving have made all of their work worthwhile. Their businesses are generating revenue at a level they find acceptable. This level of income may vary from rep to rep. But the psychic rewards are similar. There is a growing sensation of confidence, momentum, and growth. Hope has now become certainty. And doubt has been replaced with increasing determination. The vision is bigger, the task is easier, and the work is more profitable and enjoyable.

There is only one caution I would give to reps in Stage Two. Don't slow down. Many reps begin to confuse early momentum with critical mass. They are not remotely related. Early momentum is still fragile, and it needs to be sustained, managed, and fueled. Critical mass, on the other hand, is the point in physics where outside energy is no longer needed to sustain a reaction. In business it is dangerous to ever assume that a point of critical mass has been achieved.

Many reps who reach a new level of leadership are tempted to slow down and let their downlines create growth and wealth for them. They begin to manage their teams instead of continuing the same things that created their success - sticking with the basics and showing the business presentation to as many people as possible. We forget the law of sowing and reaping. We start to sow more sparingly and then become perplexed when our harvest is not abundant. The reason I know about this mistake is because I have made it.

STAGE #3: I'M NOT WORTH THIS MUCH!

I have nothing to say to those reps who are in Stage Three. I am not there yet. And for those who have made it, I simply give you my respect and honor. I am your student. I would not presume to teach you.

Lastly, I would like to clarify one thing. The description I have used for Stage Three is, "I'm not worth this much!" It is a statement that represents the thoughts of many entrepreneurs who have succeeded. It reflects their humility and their dismay at how much money can be made in a network marketing endeavor. But in practical terms, I do not agree with the statement. Entrepreneurs in network marketing, no matter how staggering the monthly sums will be in the future, are worth every dollar that comes to them. If you doubt this, then you are not thinking in entrepreneurial time. You are thinking in linear time again, "work for one hour and get paid for one hour."

As numerous men and women in network marketing begin to make millions of dollars per year (and, for some, millions of dollars per month) how can I say that they are worth this much? Entrepreneurs are not paid on an hourly basis for their productivity. They are paid for their vision, courage, and stamina. They are paid for being willing to do what others would not do. They are paid for staring down fear, ignoring fatigue, fighting loneliness, pushing through discouragement, and walking by faith. They are paid for putting their dreams, lives, and security on the line. And only those who have been there understand that being an entrepreneur is a high wire act without a safety net. They are modern day heroes who deserve everything that comes their way. I salute them.

Part Two:

THE
PSYCHOLOGICAL
SIDE OF SUCCESS

CHAPTER
SIX

THE LAST STRONGHOLD
OF DOUBT: THE SELF

Surrounded by the disarray and eclectic mix of junk so common to antique stores, the vase was nearly lost on the table. The dust and dirt suggested it had been on the table for a long time; it had no shine, no apparent beauty, and no hint of exceptional uniqueness or value. So it remained on the table, not meriting a second look by an endless stream of shoppers.

Finally, a tall, blonde woman with a patrician air about her, stopped, looked at the vase, and picked it up. She wondered if the intricate design would be more apparent if she cleaned the vase. Glancing first to the right, then to the left, she discreetly licked her thumb for moisture and began to rub the vase. Even in the dim light of the antique shop, she noticed enough improvement to give her some hope that this vase might clean up nicely. So she paid the owner three dollars and walked out the door with her purchase. When she got home, she began to clean the vase. She sat in quiet awe as its hidden beauty emerged. Its design, crafting, and color were exquisite. Curious about what she had found, she later took the vase to a specialist. After a brief study, the fine arts appraiser told her the vase had belonged to one of the Czars of Russia. He set its value at more than $50,000.

This story is repeated every day. Objects of extraordinary beauty and worth are overlooked and undervalued. But this oversight is not limited to the realm of vases. It happens all too often in the world of vessels ... human vessels. One of the silent tragedies in daily life is the number of people who dismiss themselves from being players in the game of life. In network marketing this means there is one final area of doubt we all must face. It is our belief about ourselves.

What Matters Most

It does not matter how much intellectual confidence someone has about network marketing's becoming a primary means of transacting business. It does not matter how much conviction they have about a particular network marketing company. And it does not matter how passionate they are about the compensation potential, or the quality of the products or services provided. If their belief about themselves is full of self-doubt and negativity, then this belief system will outrank and overshadow all of their confidence, conviction, and passion. In fact, it will prevent many from ever getting started in network marketing.

Others will get started but the weight of their self-doubt will keep slowing them down. For them it is like trying to drive a car with the parking brake on. They recognize that network marketing is a vehicle that could literally change their lives and financial future, but the constant drag of self-doubt prevents them from driving their businesses with abandon. They want to go forward; they believe in the business; they see its potential, and they honestly intend to stick with it. Eventually, however, the fatigue of carrying their negative belief systems into their businesses exhausts them. So they slow down. They stop pushing. They rest. And immediately the relief of rest feels much easier than the fight to carry this ever-present weight of self-doubt. So they "park" their vehicles of opportunity. They disqualify themselves from the race of life. And they settle for being a spectator.

I feel sadness for people who do this. Their faulty belief systems preclude them from success and increases the likelihood of failure. They get caught in repetitive patterns of avoidance, false starts, and failed finishes. These mistakes, in turn, only give them a larger data base of historical evidence to support their originally erroneous belief systems. Paradoxically, they become *confident* in their beliefs that they have no right to live life with confidence. They are more certain than ever that they are not entitled, qualified, or likely to ever be a winner in life. So instead of living life with abandon, they begin to abandon life. They begin to lay down their dreams and lose hope. They start to "accept their lot in life" and acquiesce to their present circumstances.

I have seen countless people do this. They determine what they will do in life by making sure that it does not require them to step outside the limits of their comfort zones and their belief systems. They are like a dog that has been trained to stay in a yard that has no fences. No matter what happens the dog will not step outside the perimeter of its yard. The dog may see the world beyond. It may even be tempted to experience it. But in the end it will remain within the confines of the yard. It unquestioningly believes that running beyond the known boundary will be unsafe, unwise, or unacceptable. In the world of dogs, this is fine. But in the world of human beings, it is tragic. Too many people live fenced in and confined by the tiny limits of their beliefs. They see a world of unlimited opportunity "over yonder" but never give themselves permission to run and play in it.

I recently saw a vivid demonstration of how limiting self-doubt can be. I watched a small group of people listen to an excellent in-home presentation about a network marketing company. When the speaker finished, a gentleman spoke up and said, "I like everything that I have

> **"Our core beliefs are the epicenter from which our thoughts, behaviors, and emotions flow."**

seen. But there is one problem. I have identified the weakest link in the chain. It is me. There is no reason why anyone should listen to me." Immediately I felt sadness for this dear man who lived with such limiting beliefs, but I respected his courage and honesty which helped him speak so forthrightly. The last stronghold of doubt...the self, had claimed another victim. His life was at a crossroads. As he hesitated at the intersection of old beliefs and new opportunity, his old beliefs prevented him from taking advantage of the new opportunity. He doesn't know it, but his beliefs will keep him living on a dead-end street.

Everyone has a unique world view and perception about their place in the world and will bring these perceptions into network marketing. Their old beliefs, expectations, and attitudes are brought directly into the company with which they affiliate. For those who dismiss themselves as mere three-dollar vessels, the most difficult aspect of growing their businesses is not learning about their company and its compensation structure. It is ensuring that their old beliefs, attitudes, and habits do not contaminate new opportunities. For these people, bringing their old mentality of negative and erroneous beliefs into their new network marketing businesses will poison their chance of success, just as it has, or will, poison every other opportunity exposed to it.

(Keep in perspective that all of us have *moments* of doubt. We may doubt ourselves, our stamina, our skill, our team, our confidence in network marketing, our company, etc. These temporary doubts are normal and okay. What is important about moments of doubt is their *frequency*, their *duration*, and their *intensity*. There is a significant difference between a brief passing thought and a belief system or mindset that is entrenched, embraced, and acted upon.)

DISCOVERING OUR BELIEF SYSTEMS

As people begin to explore their belief systems they need a starting point. I suggest it is important to pay attention to several related questions:

1. What do I believe?
2. How long have I believed this?
3. How did this belief get installed?
4. Is what I believe true, accurate, and helpful?
5. What impact will this belief have on my life if I don't change it?

How Do They Get the Jelly Inside the Doughnut?

When was the last time you had a jelly-filled doughnut? When I was a kid I loved jelly-filled doughnuts. I used to wonder, "How do they get the jelly on the inside?" (Now, as an adult, I wonder how I ever put so many of those doughnuts inside of me.) Our beliefs are like jelly-filled doughnuts. We need to explore *what* we believe and *how our beliefs got inside of us.*

Exploring these two components of our beliefs is very useful. It will also determine our future in network marketing and will reveal much about why we currently think, live, and behave as we do. Why is this? Because our core beliefs are the constitution we live by, the final law of the land. In aviation terms, they are the flight plan filed at the beginning of every flight. The destination is predetermined. In card game terminology, our beliefs are the ultimate trump card. They will beat whatever they come up against. That is why, in network marketing circles, you will occasionally hear, "A person's business will never outgrow his or her self-image."

The point is clear: our core beliefs are the epicenter from which our thoughts, behaviors, and emotions flow. When people begin to give themselves permission to explore their belief systems, they are beginning to take charge of their lives. The reason for this is simple: Either you will learn to capture your thoughts or your thoughts will capture you.

Allow me to reiterate once more the role and power of belief systems. In life, as well as in the world of network marketing, many people are never released to take advantage of extraordinary opportunities because *they are held captive by their own erroneous thinking.* Their beliefs control their behaviors; their attitudes determine their actions. The content of their thoughts dictates the quality and the conduct of their lives. The old premise that "ideas have consequences" is true.

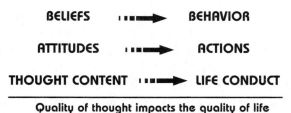

BELIEFS ⁙➡	BEHAVIOR
ATTITUDES ⁙➡	ACTIONS
THOUGHT CONTENT ⁙➡	LIFE CONDUCT

Quality of thought impacts the quality of life

Paying Attention to Our Own Beliefs

Most people live without ever questioning their core beliefs. They may know what they believe. But they have never pondered *why* they believe what they believe. They don't know precisely *when* they began to believe it, and they don't wonder if *what* they believe is true. In other words, they have no idea how the jelly got in the doughnut. That is, they have no awareness of *how* their beliefs got into their minds.

This is understandable because most people have lived with their beliefs for so long they no longer even notice them. Their thought patterns are so ingrained and so familiar they have become reflexive ways of thinking. Their minds are set, as if on autopilot, and they see no need to examine the thoughts that float across the radar screens of their minds.

Let's consider a simple illustration to demonstrate how each of us does this. Have you ever spent a day on the beach in a resort area? Often there will be a small plane flying up and down the beach towing a sign that says something like "Eat at Larry's Steakhouse." Initially we stop what we are doing and strain to read the sign. But eventually, once we become familiar with the image of the plane and its ad, we no longer pay attention to its input.

All of us do this with our thoughts. Our thoughts about ourselves, life, and the world have floated across the screens of our minds so many times we no longer pay attention to them. We take them for granted and go on about our business. This casual indifference to our own thoughts can be useful when our thought patterns are healthy and accurate. But when our thinking becomes skewed in some vital area of life, we need the ability to manage a thought before it manages us. Otherwise, like a virus in a software program, a thought can damage our ability to effectively process and respond to life.

> *"Either you will learn to capture your thoughts or your thoughts will capture you."*

Paying attention to our thoughts and belief systems can greatly enhance the growth of our businesses. To make this happen, we need to pay attention to those thoughts that keep floating across the screens of our minds. We must train ourselves to be good listeners to our own internal dialogues. In short, those thoughts that have become so familiar that they just slip in "under the radar" must be detected and evaluated for their accuracy and helpfulness. That is because, as previously stated, we will either learn to control our thoughts or our thoughts will control us.

Adjust the Volume on the Cassette Tape

Most people have never learned to pay attention to their thoughts and belief systems. But our belief systems are relatively easy to detect because we express them all the time. In the privacy of our own minds we express our belief systems in solitary, internal dialogues. (Usually at a speed of over 700 words per minute.)

To understand this process better, picture the mind as a cassette tape on continuous play. Our beliefs are recorded on this cassette tape and are playing back to us constantly. However, this tape's volume level is quite low, and to hear it we have to listen attentively. As people learn to do this, it gets easier to "hear" what is on the tape. They can now know what they are saying to themselves. This puts them in a position to evaluate the veracity and the impact of their own beliefs on their lives.

Learn to eavesdrop on your own mind. You will be amazed at the things that you regularly *think, feel,* and *say to yourself.* Do your thoughts throw another log on the fire of confidence, or do they quench your motivation and courage? Do they inspire you to believe in yourself and attempt new challenges, or do they talk you out of getting involved with anything that is outside of your comfort zone? Do your most influential thoughts whisper to you or shout at you? Some people need to turn the volume up on the cassette tape of their minds, and others need to turn it down.

Here are some things to listen for on the cassette tape of your own mind:

- *Is what I say to myself:*
    -helpful

    -positive

    -constructive

    -motivating

    -kind

    -inspiring

-Does this engender:
- -self confidence
- -optimism
- -delight
- -perseverance
- -personal strength
- -hope
- -trust in myself
- -trust in my business
- -laughter
- -freedom to succeed
- -freedom to fail
- -freedom to attempt new things
- -freedom to learn new things
- -freedom to speak up
- -freedom to dream
- -freedom to risk new behaviors
- -freedom to lead
- -freedom to serve
- -freedom to grow my business

As you consider the above list, what kinds of things are you repeatedly saying to or about yourself? Which thoughts do you want to keep and which ones will keep you from growing? Can you identify when these thoughts got "installed" or put onto the cassette tape? Can you identify the source of these thoughts? (With practice, many people can literally hear the voice, volume, and tone of the person who initially installed the thought that has now become recorded as a life belief.)

Fragile Egos and Bruised Peaches

Do you remember what many of us were taught as children to say when other kids were unkind to us? We used to respond with: "Sticks and stones will break my bones but names will never hurt me." It is a cute retort for kids. Unfortunately, it is not completely true. Words wield enormous power; they can literally shape, make, and break a life. No wonder the writer of Proverbs wrote, "Death and life are in the power of the tongue and those who love it will eat its fruits." He also wrote, "Pleasant words are like honeycomb, sweetness to the soul, and health to the body."

What others say to, or about us can be very influential. This is why Bob Torsey, a compelling trainer in a premier network marketing company, teaches that everyone has fragile egos. He kiddingly reminds us that our egos are like peaches. If you bump a peach, four hours later it will have a bruise. In living our lives and growing our businesses we will all be bruised by others. This is an unavoidable part of life in the real world.

If you are going to thrive while growing your network marketing business, you have to become tough enough to live with bruises others give you. But you also need to be sure that you are not creating your own bruises. What kinds of things do *you* say to yourself? Do these thoughts and words bring life, health, vigor, and determination? Or are they words of death that can leave you bruised and demotivated?

I am amazed at the number of adults who have matured enough to speak words of grace and kindness to others, *yet have never learned to speak words of grace and kindness to themselves.* They cut themselves no slack, give themselves no vote of confidence, allow themselves no margin for error, and expect themselves to be perfect in all they do. When taken to an extreme, this over-demanding self-talk is counterproductive. It either prevents individuals from succeeding or, if they do succeed, they are never free to enjoy their own success.

You Gotta Be Mentally Tough!

In growing a business it is especially important for individuals to be able to manage their own self-talk, which will impact their management of pressure and conflict. It will influence their response to setbacks and failure, and will play a role in how they handle success, notoriety, leadership, speaking, and management. In short, no aspect of their businesses will be exempt from the power of self-talk.

This is why individuals in network marketing must learn to be mentally tough. They need the ability to stay focused, on-task, and undeterred no matter what is happening around them. *I believe this is the most important and the most difficult aspect of growing any business, especially a network marketing business.* In those inevitable moments when people are tempted to doubt, quit, or take the easy way out, their clarity of thought and mental toughness can keep them going. It allows them to keep working, dreaming, and believing. It allows them to persevere and stay tethered to their dreams and objectives. Finally, it enables them to ignore the cacophony of other thoughts taunting them to lay down their dreams and let go of this foolish notion that they could develop a successful business in network marketing.

This ability to stay mentally focused, tough, and confident is most important in the early stages of starting our businesses. All that keeps us going in the beginning is the power of an idea and the hope of success. Initially, we have no tangible "proof" to assure others or ourselves that this endeavor will work in the end. It is a season of life where we have to walk by faith and not by sight. As people learn to live in entrepreneurial time they accept this ambiguity and even find excitement in it. Their ability to "see" the future gives them confidence in the present. But those whose self-talk is punctuated with doubt, distrust, and caution are susceptible to talking themselves out of their own success. Similarly, those who want life to be predictable, scripted, and with a minimal amount of uncertainty will be most tempted to give up and fall back into the familiar life they know with its lower levels of uncertainty and stress...but with no hope of great change, success, or achievement.

Tips for Mental Toughness

One characteristic is common to men and women who remain focused and mentally tough in network marketing: they accept responsibility for the management of their own minds. This is why reading, listening to quality tapes, and associating with colleagues who are equally focused is a natural way of life for them. Knowing that ideas have consequences, they do whatever is necessary to insure that:

1. Their vision is clear.
2. Their motivation is high.
3. Their skills are ever increasing.

To newcomers, network marketing veterans may appear overly zealous. They constantly seem to be reading books, listening to motivational tapes, and attending meetings. In reality, what these veterans understand is that dreams, courage, and motivation need tending like a garden. They know the mind is the soil where thoughts are planted. They know it is the seedbed from which life emerges. And they are committed to protecting the soil of their minds and planting healthy thoughts. What develops over time is a human being who has blossomed, a business that is growing, and many other lives that have been changed. This is the great power and joy of network marketing that often goes unnoticed.

So What About You?

We have used many word pictures in this chapter. Let me review some of them briefly:

- vases and vessels that are overlooked and undervalued.
- self-doubt that slows people down, as if they were driving a car with the parking brake on.
- dogs and people fenced in by the imaginary limitations of their own perceptions about the world and their places in it.
- installed beliefs, like jelly in a doughnut, which can profoundly influence a person's sense of worth and potential.
- a plane towing a sign that represents thoughts that float across the screens of our minds.
- cassette tapes on continuous replay illustrating how our beliefs are continually expressed, even if we no longer consciously notice them.
- egos that get bruised like peaches.
- soil and gardens that need planting and tending.

As you consider your life, what are some of your beliefs? What kind of place do you think the world is? What do you think is your place in the world? Do you believe you have the right to be a player in the game of life instead of a spectator? Do you think you are capable of success in network marketing? Can you give yourself permission to risk new endeavors and attempt new areas of growth and accomplishment? Do you recognize that getting involved in network marketing is not just an invitation to grow a business and earn some income, but is actually an invitation to take responsibility for, and be in charge of, your future and your life?

For some people, this is the time to stop selling themselves so cheaply. It is time to stop viewing themselves as a "three-dollar vase." It is time to stop being constrained by their own limited thinking. It is time to look at the jelly in the doughnut and see what beliefs have been installed. It is time to listen to the cassette tapes of their minds. It is time to see the thoughts that keep floating across the screens of their minds. It is time to realize their minds are like their own personal gardens, and that it is their privilege and responsibility to tend them. It is time to give themselves permission to think for themselves. It is time to think thoughts that are true, healthy, and empowering. It is time to perceive themselves as winners in the game of life. It is their time. It is their turn. Like Tiger Woods, they need to realize they are ready for the world and then discover if the world is ready for them.

CHAPTER SEVEN

PUTTING NEW JELLY INSIDE AN OLD DOUGHNUT

I t was the same question I always ask. She and her sister have heard it countless times. By now they're bored with the whole thing, so when I ask the question, they laugh and roll their eyes. But I keep asking it anyway.

This night was no exception. I was saying goodnight to my eleven-year-old daughter. We sat on her bed while we talked, snuggled, and laughed. As I got up to leave I looked directly into her eyes and did it again. I held her face in my hands and said, "Hey! I've got a question for you! What is it like to be eleven years old and loved by your dad?" She sighed and grinned and gave a typical response for an eleven-year-old, "It's nice, Dad." With that I told her I loved her, stroked her face, kissed her good night, and I was gone.

Why do I keep asking a question that my daughters pretend bores them? Because each time I do it I am putting jelly into the doughnut. I am installing and reinforcing a belief that allows them to close out one day and begin another with the fresh knowledge that they are loved. No matter how old we are, these are strong bookends for a day.

As we grow older, and particularly as we grow our network marketing businesses, the jelly in our doughnuts will be revealed. Our beliefs and expectations about life will be pushed to the surface from the normal pressures of building our businesses. Some of these beliefs will greatly enhance the growth of our businesses. At other times, we'll find jelly in the doughnuts that hinders success.

Changing The Jelly

When people begin to pay attention to the jelly in the doughnut, they inevitably want to know: What do I do with those thoughts, feelings, beliefs, and behaviors that are not to my liking? What do I do with the installed beliefs? How do I really change the cassette tape that is always playing? How do I monitor the thoughts that float across the screen of my mind?

What they want to know is, "How do I change the jelly that is in the doughnut?" It is not just a matter of emptying out the old jelly. Some other jelly that is true, healthy, and empowering has to be injected into the doughnut. *This is because winning the mental battle for success in life and network marketing does not come from the absence of negative beliefs. It comes from the presence of core beliefs and thinking habits that are true, positive, and empowering.*

Let's look at the two aspects of changing the jelly in the doughnut: First, we must identify the unwanted jelly and determine how it got put into the doughnut. Second, we have to figure out how to put new jelly into the doughnut.

Learning to Identify Different Types of Jelly

To help a person recognize his or her own thinking style, I recommend listening carefully to the people they interact with each day. It is a great way to learn how to identify thought patterns that have enormous consequences, even when thoughts seem to be expressed casually.

Listen to those around you and pay attention to the core beliefs and thought patterns they reveal about themselves. You will be amazed at what they disclose about their belief systems. You will notice what they think, say, and feel about themselves and life. Without even knowing it, they will tell you the kind of jelly that is in their doughnuts. They will let you hear the tape that plays in their minds. Notice how often you will hear someone casually begin a sentence with:

- I could never do...
- I'm no good at...
- I'm not very...
- I always...
- I'm too ....
- I would like to, but...

Each of these introductions will be followed by the jelly that is in their doughnuts. You will hear the self-limiting and self-dismissing beliefs they have about themselves. They are about to disclose that they have *too little* or *too much* of something. In either case they are telling you their core beliefs. They are also inferring that their core beliefs make it reasonable for them not to expect to succeed. It does not occur to them to challenge their own thinking. They have lived with these beliefs for so long they no longer even question them. They may not like them, but they no longer fight them. They have given in to them. Whether or not they are true, reasonable, or accurate no longer matters.

Following are some of the beliefs that you can listen for.

THE *I'M NOT* BELIEFS

- *not smart enough*	- *not educated enough*
- *not funny enough*	- *not friendly enough*
- *not outgoing enough*	- *not poised enough*
- *not disciplined enough*	- *not confident enough*
- *not tenacious enough*	- *not talented enough*
- *not tough enough*	- *not mature enough*
- *not good with numbers*	- *not good with details*
- *not a good leader*	- *not a good speaker*
- *not a good planner*	- *not a good motivator*
- *not a good manager*	- *not a good person*

The above are statements people commonly use to describe themselves and explain why they are not likely to attempt or succeed in something.

Let's personalize the above list. Which of the above do you think, feel, believe, and say about *yourself?* These are the beliefs, or jelly that determine what your life and business become.

Once you identify a negative thought pattern, the next step is to decide what you want to do about it. (It can either continue to control you or you can begin to control it.) I suggest that you keep some of the following steps in mind:

1. Identify the jelly in the doughnut. (The belief you want to change.)

2. Ask, "Who told you that?" (Identify how or when it got installed.)

3. Fire some old coaches. (Give yourself permission to challenge and change unhealthy beliefs.)

4. Put new jelly in the doughnut. (Embrace new thought patterns that are healthy, true, and empowering.)

WHO TOLD YOU THAT?

If I had the privilege of being with you personally, together we would begin to identify the jelly in your doughnut. We would begin to discover the beliefs that float across the screen of your mind, those that set you free and those that become limitations on your life and business. At some point, when I heard you disclose a core belief that limits you, I would inquire: "Where did you learn to believe that? Who told you that?" Together we would begin to explore how and when that belief got installed. Let's look at some examples of other people to demonstrate how jelly gets put into the doughnut.

Sarah: She grew up in a home where she and her siblings were constantly told they were loved and that they could do or become whatever they wanted in life. This belief was installed and reinforced for years. Today, Sarah is in network marketing because she is an entrepreneur. She loves the freedom of network marketing, and she is not afraid of either success or failure.

Frank: He is one of the most multitalented people I know. He has a keen mind and remarkable auditory recall. He is also an extremely hard worker and wonderful with people. However, it doesn't matter that I know and believe this because Frank does not really believe it.

What jelly is in his doughnut? What plays on his cassette tape? He keeps hearing his father's repetitious warning from years ago: "If you don't start doing better in school you are going to end up with a shovel digging ditches."

His father, with good motives, attempted to motivate his son with fear and shame. Unfortunately, Frank has dyslexia that went unnoticed in school. Continuous messages of fear and shame could not fix this visual-perceptual problem. Ironically, Frank drives an earth mover today. It is nothing more than an expensive shovel. His loving father had inadvertently dug the very hole he was trying to keep his son out of. He installed a belief that became Frank's self-fulfilling prophecy. What is exciting is that Frank is now involved in building a network marketing business. He is giving himself permission to ignore what plays on his tape. Instead, he is daring to dream, willing to work, and ready to change his life.

FIRE SOME OLD COACHES

Identifying the jelly in the doughnut is the easy part. The more challenging task is learning to over-rule negative beliefs so they no longer rule over you. It is accepting responsibility for the thoughts that float across the screen of your mind. It is taking charge of the cassette player and choosing what you will listen to. It is appointing yourself as master chef and determining what jelly you will accept. It is giving yourself permission to explore your beliefs. Like David challenging Goliath, this is your opportunity to run out and conquer the habitual beliefs and behaviors that will hold you captive if you don't deal with them.

At times, we have to "fire some old coaches". We release some people from having so much power over us. These people might be a friend, colleague, spouse, sibling, parent, teacher, coach, etc. They might be living, or they might be dead. They may live near you or far away. But in each case they have injected a negative belief into your mind that currently interferes with your ability to be your best. A couple of examples might help.

Jim: We have been friends for twenty years. I met Jim in college where he was a straight "A" student. Upon graduation he went to work for IBM and then another computer company. Wherever he went he was a star performer who became the best at what he did. Everyone admired and appreciated his prodigious talent, hard work, and well-earned success. Every one but him. He never savored his own success. He always found some fault with his performance. He always disappointed himself.

One day, over a cup of coffee, I asked Jim how he got so good at making himself feel so bad. How did he develop the habit of working so hard and then being disappointed with outstanding results? For his sake, I wanted to know how the jelly got in the doughnut. I wanted to know when and how he adopted the belief that he is always a disappointment. I wanted to know, *"Who told you that?"*

Jim began to share that when he was growing up he was an exceptionally gifted swimmer. For years he was much taller and stronger than any of the competitors his age. He swam competitively and set numerous state and local records. Everyone assumed Jim was destined to be an Olympic swimmer. But in his last years of high school, he was no longer bigger and stronger than all of his competitors. Some of them caught up with him. He was very good but he was not great.

One day in swimming practice, Jim pulled himself out of the pool. As he looked up, his varsity swimming coach was standing right in front of him. The coach had his arms folded across his chest and was shaking his head from side to side as he looked at Jim with disgust. Finally he said, "I don't get it. I don't know how anyone can have so much talent and yet do so poorly!" *BANG!* The jelly was injected. In that moment the coach, in his authoritative position, installed a core belief. He loaded the cassette tape with a message that pulled rank over everything else Jim thought, did, or heard from others. The message was clear: You are nothing but a huge disappointment.

Jim identified the negative core belief that he had been living with. He also gave himself permission to no longer allow the coach's unwise comment to have such influence in his life. He learned to control the volume on the cassette tape and to capture that painful thought when it floated across his mind. In short, he fired the coach. He relieved the coach from the negative influence and power he had held over him for so long. Today, Jim continues to be exceptionally productive, successful, and wealthy. The difference is that he is now free to enjoy his own success.

It is vital for you to discover your core beliefs and give yourself permission to challenge the toxic beliefs or people that poison your ability to believe in yourself. Avoiding this keeps many people out of the winners' circle in network marketing. Or it precludes them from enjoying their own achievements. I have spent thousands of hours with senators, congresspersons, generals, admirals, world class athletes, and corporate executives who were unable to enjoy their own extraordinary accomplishments because they had never learned to explore, challenge, and change their faulty core beliefs. The toxic jelly in their doughnut took the joy out of life until they learned to change it.

HOW TO CHANGE THE JELLY IN A DOUGHNUT

At this point some of you may be thinking, "Tom, I know what my core beliefs are! I know which ones are healthy and which ones aren't. I know how they got installed! And I want to challenge and change them! But I am not having as much success as I want. Can you explain this?"

For some people the answer lies in the fact that they have only learned to identify how beliefs got *injected* into their minds. But they don't know how to *eject* core beliefs *from* their minds. Additionally, they have nothing to take the place of their negative beliefs and thought patterns. (It is like knowing how to put a cassette tape into a tape deck but not knowing how to get it out. And, if you get it out, not having another tape to replace it.)

This is why I said earlier that, "winning the mental battle for success in life and network marketing does not come from the absence of negative beliefs. It comes from the presence of core beliefs and habits of thinking that are true, positive, and empowering."

So how do you eject unhealthy core beliefs and thought patterns from the screen of your mind? I'd like to answer the question without boring you with the details of neuropsychology and cognition. Instead, I'll use two word pictures: a slide projector and the remote control for your television. (These word pictures are based on the assumption that someone does not have a biochemical imbalance which makes the management of thoughts and emotions much more difficult without proper nutrition and/or medication.)

The Slide Projector

All that is needed for a slide show is a projector, slides, and a button that controls the ejection and insertion of slides. Our minds work in much the same way. A rough approximation would be: The projector is like our brain. The slides are the thoughts and images on the screen of our mind, and the control button is our decision-making ability. The projector can only show one slide at a time. There may be another hundred slides ready to go, but only one slide gets to be displayed front and center. Our minds work like this too. Only one thought or image at a time gets to be displayed prominently on the screens of our minds.

The good news is that we get to be the choreographer of our own slide show. We get to determine what thoughts and images will be projected onto the screens of our minds. We also get to decide how long they will remain on the screen.

Do you remember times when someone invited you to see "just a few slides" of their family or vacation? I would instantly try to calculate the number of slides they had and how long it would take to show and talk about each slide. I wanted to know just how long this "privilege" was going to last. I would be thinking, "Let's see, sixty slides with an average explanation of fifty seconds. . .Oh no! I think I better get a cup of coffee." I felt stuck because I

> **"Success comes from core beliefs and thinking habits that are true, positive, and empowering."**

had no control over what slides would be projected onto the screen and how long they would remain there.

Curiously, some people live with the sensation of being at the mercy of someone else's slide presentation. They don't know how to monitor the thoughts, images, and associated feelings that float across the screens of their own minds. It never occurs to them that the projector, slides, and control button all belong to them. It is their choice and responsibility to determine what is viewed.

These people remind me of a friend of mine. I recently borrowed his slide projector to do a business presentation. After I returned it to him he called me and mentioned that the remote control button with its twenty-foot extension cord was missing. I felt bad and told him that

I would gladly do whatever was necessary to replace the missing control. Several weeks later we discovered the control button and its cord. It had been placed into a side panel on the projector. Right where it belonged. It was not visible but it was there all along.

Some people live as if the control buttons for the slide projectors of their minds have been misplaced. Thoughts, images, memories, or fears keep floating across the screen, and they feel powerless to control or change them. They don't know where the control button is. They don't realize that they have the ability to monitor any of their thoughts, that they can eject them from the projector and insert better slides. As a result, rather than controlling the images of their minds, the images of their minds control them. They are now at the mercy of the images and all of the thoughts and emotions associated with them. All because they have never learned the art of being the choreographers of their own slide shows. They did not know it was within their powers to remove negative slides and replace them with others that are more useful.

To demonstrate how to control or change those images on the screens of our minds, let's switch word pictures. Let's use the remote control for our television and video player. In fact, if you have one handy, it would be useful to go and get it before you read this section.

The Mighty Remote Control

You know the old joke about the golden rule: He or she who has the gold... rules. In many homes today there is a parallel thought: He or she who has the remote control rules.

What is so much fun about holding the remote control? It gives the person holding it the sensation of being in control and calling the shots. They become the master of the universe and determine what stays and what gets zapped away. Why not learn how to use the remote control as an analogy for monitoring our lives and thoughts? That is real power and mastery. Not temporary illusion.

Look at, or imagine, your remote control. What are some of the control buttons that you notice? The ones that are useful for our purposes are:

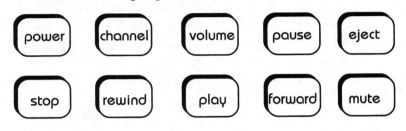

What a great menu of choices. These same choices are available to us in our thoughts. Knowing how to use them can change our lives and our businesses. Proper use of the remote control will keep us motivated, confident, and tenacious in growing our businesses. It will make us strong, and then it will make us successful.

Here is how it works. Select a negative belief that you would like to change. Pick one that is important. In fact, choose one that is so important that you know if you do not correct it, it will rob you of achieving your business potential.

After you identify the core belief or habitual thought that you would like to change, ask yourself some questions about it. Don't shy away from this belief. Begin to give yourself permission to understand it. Begin to study it. Become an authority on it. Ask yourself these questions:

- What specific negative belief would I like to change?
- Why is it important that I change it?

- What will happen if I don't begin to face and change this belief?
- What would I like to replace this belief with?
- How long have I lived with this belief?
- Do I know when and how it got installed?
- Did this belief get installed in an instant? (Like Jim's belief installed by his swimming coach.)
- Did this belief get injected in small but repeated doses that eventually became poisonous? (Like Frank's father with his repeated warnings based on fear.)
- When this negative belief fills my mind, is it mostly visual or auditory? Do I see it or hear it? Is it the image or the sound that carries the most impact?
- If it is auditory, is it loud and overwhelming, coming at me like a digitized Dolby sound system? Or is it insidiously quiet like the hiss of a snake about to strike?

After pondering some of these preliminary questions, give yourself permission to determine what is acceptable viewing in the theater of your mind. Become the manager of your own theater. Make yourself the boss. Be your own Siskel and Ebert. If you deem that something on the screen of your mind is unhealthy and inappropriate, then change it. You don't have to passively sit there and watch junk on the screen of your mind.

Pick up the remote control and become the master of your universe. Learn to zap those images that you don't want. Change the channel. Eject the video. If you are listening to thoughts that steal your joy and confidence, then hit the mute button! Turn down the volume. If you need a minute to decide just what you want to do, then hit the pause button. If you cannot think of anything good to watch, then hit the stop button. Turn off the power. The choice is yours. You can decide what is acceptable viewing and listening for you.

INSERTING NEW TAPES INTO THE VCR

In the management of your mind, learning how to turn down the volume on the cassette tapes becomes a powerful tool. It is very useful to know how to eject negative images from the screens of our minds. However it is also necessary to have something to replace these. When you stop watching one slide or video on the screen of your mind you need to replace it with another. Similarly, you don't want to just turn down the volume on negative tapes that play. You want to literally replace them with new tapes that are true, healthy, and empowering.

The goal is to change the jelly in the doughnut. You want the core beliefs and habits of thought to be true and empowering. You want a mindset that instills confidence and vision. You want to know that you have what it takes to be a player in the game of life and in the world of network marketing. You want the tapes, images, and videos that play in your mind to be those of a winner. This way, when moments of doubt come while building your business, you just keep going, working, building, and believing. You remain determined and undaunted as you work on making your own dreams become a reality.

Future Rehearsals

There are many ways that people create new tapes and images in their minds. For example, you can use all of your senses (sight, sound, smell, touch, and taste) while picturing your upcoming success. It may be rehearsing in your mind the making of an acceptance speech, receiving an award, cashing checks, purchasing some new items, giving money to charity to help others, etc. There is a place for all of these. They are helpful because they flood you with the strong positive emotions associated with the images you select.

In effect, these images allow you to experience *in the present* the state of well being that will accompany your success *in the future*. They are called "future rehearsals". And you already know how to do them. Millions of people are masters at living in a time frame we call the present, while experiencing the emotions of something they envision in the future. Unfortunately they use this great skill only to work against themselves. It is commonly called anxiety, worry, or dread.

What these people do is take a sneak preview of their imagined future. They picture in full color and great detail all the bad things that can happen to them. They create movies in their minds that make Steven Speilberg look like an amateur film maker. As these movies are created and then watched over and over, they have their desired effect. They scare the daylights out of the person watching them.

Imagine using this same skill and creating films that create future rehearsals of being tenacious, working hard, overcoming obstacles, being successful, and winning. Now that is a film worth watching! Create your own images and movies that inspire you and play them on the screen of your mind. When you have done this, then I suggest you get comfortable, make some popcorn, and grab the remote. Hit play, turn up the volume, and enjoy the show.

Creating Videos About Who You Are.... Already

When some people review the cassette tapes or videos of their minds, they cannot find many that are positive. They don't have memories of a parent tucking them into bed while telling them that they are loved, special, and believed in. The jelly in their doughnuts is not that sweet. What should they do? While identifying, challenging and changing old tapes that are not true, I suggest that they become aware of some other realities that are true, healthy, and empowering right now. Even if they never knew them or accepted them.

I began this chapter by sharing with you some of the beliefs and images that I want my daughters to have on the screens of their minds. May I suggest to you that this same story is already yours. It may simply be a cassette tape or video that you have never watched or taken seriously.

The idea of telling my children that I love them is not original with me. I borrowed it from the "play book" of another father. Without doubt, he is much better at being a parent than I am. He is the master chef when it comes to injecting good jelly into the doughnut with elegance. Listen to what this dad said one day while he was speaking to others about his son. In his son's presence he stated, "This is my beloved son, with whom I am well pleased. Listen to him."

Let's look at the jelly he put into the doughnut and the beliefs that he put onto the cassette tape in these two brief sentences. They are loaded with insight.

- This is *MY* beloved *SON.* With two words he is making the position, place, stature, and identity of the child perfectly clear. You are *MY CHILD.* Don't ever wonder about your place in the world.
- This is my *BELOVED* son. By using one adjective he is making it clear what he feels for this child. You are *LOVED.* Don't ever wonder about what I think and feel for you.
- With whom I am *WELL PLEASED.* With two words he set his child free for life. He let him

119

know that he already had his father's *AP-PROVAL*. Spend your life enjoying my approval rather than seeking it.

Some of you know how I became privy to this conversation and the playbook that I borrowed it from. The "playbook" is the Bible, and the speaker is the Heavenly Father. Some of you may question what this has to do with your success in network marketing. It is a fair question.

> *"You want the tapes, images, and videos that play in your mind to be those of a winner."*

Undoubtedly, the jelly in your doughnut will be revealed while you grow your business. Your beliefs about life, others, and yourself will all come to the surface. Your capacity to maintain entrepreneurial vision, clear focus, and daily discipline will be tested. There will be stretches of road where you feel alone. The people around you will not know, care, or understand what you are doing in your business or why you are doing it. You will encounter a learning curve in the management of your business, your team, and yourself. (This is a nice way of saying that you will make numerous mistakes along the way.) Throughout all of these encounters it helps to have jelly in the doughnut that makes you resilient, confident, and tough.

Knowing the love of your Heavenly Father towards you can facilitate this.

It is enormously freeing to begin each day with cassette tapes and videos playing that remind you that you are *already* a person of dignity, deeply loved, and approved of. This will remind you that there is nothing to prove today. Rather, there is much to enjoy. When these thoughts become core beliefs, they wonderfully impact the way you start, grow, and manage your business. They will improve your disposition and your perspective while you work each day to make your dreams become your reality.

Injecting Some Reality Into the Doughnut

In this chapter we have looked at some word pictures that are easy to understand. They are simple illustrations. But simple is not the same thing as easy. The process of identifying, challenging, and changing our core beliefs and habits of thought is a major endeavor. But like growing a network marketing business, it is worth the work.

In the end, the most challenging aspect of managing your business will be the management of your mind. This is why the most successful people in network marketing take the management of their thought life so seriously. They understand the proverb, "As a man thinketh in his heart...so is he." Consequently, they regularly put themselves in a position to have their mind renewed, their vision restored, and their will strengthened. It is the reason they are avid readers, listen to tapes, and associate with other positive individuals. They consistently develop a mindset that sets them up for success.

As for you, monitor the jelly that is in your doughnut as if your life and future depend upon it. They do.

CHAPTER EIGHT

I'LL BE THE DESIGNATED DRIVER

Maybe you are like me. I am fascinated by the license plates that people choose to put on their cars. With just a few letters or numbers they are attempting to communicate something that is meaningful to them. I recently saw two that I loved. They were:

XPCT2WN   1GR8DAY

What marvelous messages. Imagine coming out of the chutes each day exuding an attitude of EXPECT TO WIN! How terrific to live life with the idea that this is ONE GREAT DAY! It makes you glad to be alive and ready to jump into the arena of life rather than just drag through another day. It is a wonderful way to live.

This same attitude of positive expectancy and living each day to the fullest is expressed by Whitney Houston

in the song, *"One Moment In Time."* Notice how the lyrics
awaken the inherent desire within all of us to be "more
than I thought I could be."

Each day I live I want to be
a day to give the best of me.
I'm only one but not alone;
my finest day is yet unkown.

I broke my heart for everything
to taste the sweet, oh I face the pain;
I rise and fall, yet thru it all
this much remains.

I want one moment in time
when I'm more than I, I thought I could be,
when all of my dreams are a heartbeat away,
and the answers are all up to me.

Give me one moment in time
when I'm racing with destiny,
and in that one moment of time
I will feel, I will feel, eternity.

I live to be the very best;
I want it all, no time for less.
I've laid the plans, now lay the chance
here in my hands.

Give me one, one moment in time
when I'm more than I, I thought I could be,
when all of my dreams are a heart beat away,
and the answers are all up to me.

Give me one moment in time
when I'm racing with destiny,
and in that one moment of time
I will feel, see I will feel, eternity.

You're, you're a winner
for a lifetime
if you sieze that one moment in time;
make it shine.

Give me one moment in time
when I'm more, when I'm more, than I thought I
could be,
when all of my dreams are a heartbeat away,
and the answers are all up to me.

Just give me one moment in time
when I'm racing with destiny,
and in that one moment of time
I will feel, I will feel, oh I will be free.
Yes, I will be, I will be free.

Printed with permission of Warner Bros., Publications

A song like this can stir something in our souls and ignite a longing for our own personal achievement and pride in accomplishment. Songs can inspire us to believe that the best is yet to come. The words remind us that we still long to live life with courage and abandon; they welcome us, in the arena of life, to get out of our seats as spectators and onto the field of play. There we can lay it all on the line, test our mettle, develop our skills, and use our strengths. We can know the joy of being active players and winners in life.

For most people, the longing and the inspiration end with the song. This is because the brief *feeling of inspiration* is not supported by *thoughts* that are equally inspiring. But for others, the inspiration of life turns into aspiration. For these fortunate people, strong positive feelings are coupled with equally strong thoughts. When these are fused together, a strength of will is forged resulting in action that can change a life.

How Network Marketing Fits Into This

For many people, involvement with a network marketing company is a tangible demonstration of their courageous desire to change their lives. This is why I have so much respect for people in this industry. They are risking new behaviors, they are attempting new things, and they are trying to embrace the feelings, thoughts, and behaviors that suggest that this is one great day. They expect to win, and this is their moment in time to reach higher than they have ever dared before.

In short, what they are doing is taking responsibility for their own lives. They want some measure of control over their future, so they have decided to become the CEO of their own lives.

THANK YOU, BUT I WILL DRIVE MY OWN CAR

Have you noticed the campaign to have someone be the designated driver when friends are drinking alcohol? It is a life-saving idea. At times, the most responsible thing a person can do is to allow someone else to take responsibility for his or her safety. In these moments it is an act of maturity to temporarily yield the right to drive a car. Wisely, they give their authority and power to another person.

On the other hand, I am amazed at how often I see perfectly capable people allowing others to be their designated drivers. Not just for their cars, but for major portions of their lives. They hand authority, power, decisions, or control to someone else and give others undue influence in their lives. *They habitually allow someone else to make decisions for them. Even though they are the ones who have to live with the consequences of those decisions they allow someone else to make, they keep giving their power away.*

See if you recognize the following behavior types:

Michael: He "decided" to select a major in college that made his parents proud. Unfortunately, he is not well suited to that field of study, and he is miserable. He gave his power away, and now he gets to live with the consequences.

Debbie: She "decided" to marry a man that her dad would approve of as a good choice. Regrettably, she is not well-suited to her spouse. She gave her power away, and now she, not daddy, is living with the consequences.

John: He "decided" to stay in his current job "because they need me here." Sadly, he is underpaid and increasingly frustrated with his work. He gave his power away, and now he gets to live with the consequences.

Chip and Lisa: They "decided" not to get involved with network marketing because they were unsure of what their friends would think. Unfortunately, they needed some extra income, so now they are feeling the pressure of financial constraint. They gave their power away, and now they get to live with the consequences.

Many people get involved in network marketing because they are accustomed to being their own designated drivers. They are comfortable making decisions about the direction and management of their lives. While valuing the counsel and opinions of others, they happily accept the responsibility of making their own life choices. Network marketing, for them, is a perfect environment in which to grow and manage their own businesses, pursue their dreams, leverage their time, and set their own financial goals. They wouldn't have it any other way.

If you are one of these people, be thankful. Make sure that you also remain sensitive to what it is like for others who are considering getting involved in network marketing for the first time. For some, giving themselves permission to dream is new. Acknowledging that they want their circumstances to change may be new. Daring to believe in their own potential and abilities may be new. Giving themselves permission to learn and fail while pursuing success may be new. Allowing themselves to feel hope, optimism, and pride may be a long-forgotten experience. And deciding to accept appropriate responsibility for their future may be both exhilarating and frightening to them. These people deserve our highest respect, greatest support, and finest training. They are not simply attempting to start new businesses. They are attempting to start new lives.

REALITY AS A MOTIVATOR

One important aspect of leadership and management is knowing *what* to say, *when* to say it, and *how* to say it. In my work with people there are occasions when injecting cold reality is the best thing I can do to help them. It is the only way to get some people motivated enough to get going or to keep going. Here are two realities that I might share when speaking to a group or to an individual.

1. Other people do not care if you remain dead broke.

2. You will either face the fear of doing network marketing or you will face the fear of <u>not</u> doing network marketing.

These may sound harsh to you. But they are very free-ing when understood. Let's look at them one at a time.

REALITY #1: PEOPLE DON'T CARE IF YOU REMAIN DEAD BROKE

In my work, I regularly meet professionals who are in serious financial trouble. They might be Senators, Congresspersons, physicians, attorneys, or corporate officers. But the dilemma is the same for these men and women. They are dead broke. They spend more than they make. And they are feeling the relentless bind of economic stress squeeze the joy out of life.

Some of these people, when presented with a network marketing opportunity, are very intrigued. Their business savvy lets them know that this is an efficient and effective means of growing a business. Their experiences and emotions tell them that this is something they could do with great success, and they recognize it as a way to resolve their financial struggles.

But then their pride or insecurity kicks in. The cassette tapes of their minds begin to play. They start to imagine how their friends will react. They wonder if their friends will discover that they are having financial problems. Or, they wonder if their friends will assume they have become involved in some scam that is nothing more than a pyramid scheme. (It doesn't occur to them that their friends might admire their good business sense, entrepreneurial spirit, and energy.)

For fear of their friends' reactions, they decide to decline the invitation to become involved with network marketing. When they do this, they have just given their power over to their friends. They make major decisions about their own lives based on their assumptions about what their friends might think. Unknowingly, they appoint their friends as designated drivers of their lives. (Additionally, when they do this, they are managing their social image instead of solving their problem or chasing their dreams.)

When I see someone make a decision of this sort, I will say something like this:

"Do you mind if I inject a little reality into your situation? Your friends really don't care if you are dead broke and stay that way forever. Let me share with you how their dinner conversation might go if they found out that you cannot pay your mortgage (or rent) this month.

Wife: "Hey, did you hear that Bob and Sue cannot pay their mortgage this month? Isn't that sad?"

Husband: "That really is terrible. I feel sorry for them. I hope that doesn't ever happen to us. By the way, please pass the salad."

That is about how much time they will spend lamenting your dilemma. The reasons for this are simple:

1. They assume if you are chronically broke and living on the edge of financial disaster then you must not mind it. They assume if you didn't like it then you would do something about it. Since it doesn't seem to bother you, they are not going to let it bother them.

2. They correctly know that your financial matters are your responsibility and not theirs. So, while they may *care*, they are not going to *accept responsibility* for the solution to *your* problem.

3. They are too busy trying to hold their own lives together to spend too much time worrying about yours. (Zig Ziglar is correct when he jokes that if we knew how seldom people thought of us we would stop worrying about *what* they thought of us!)

4. Your friends will struggle with your financial *success* more than they will with your financial hardships.

When people begin to grasp these realities, it frees them to stop allowing others to be their designated drivers. It motivates them to get in the driver's seat and accept responsibility for their lives and finances. They begin to make good decisions for the right reasons. Over time, they get to live with the consequences of their decisions: their lives are their own, their dreams are becoming reality, and their circumstances are positively transformed.

REALITY #2: YOU WILL EITHER FACE THE FEAR OF DOING NETWORK MARKETING, OR YOU WILL FACE THE FEAR OF <u>NOT</u> DOING NETWORK MARKETING

I recently witnessed a robbery. I saw the crime, knew the victim, and could easily identify both the thief and what was stolen. But I didn't even bother to report it to the police. They knew the thief. They knew he would strike again. And they knew there was nothing they could do to stop this crime from reoccurring. Its devastating impact on lives and its incalculable loss of money would continue unabated.

Instead of talking to the police, I talked to the victim. I told him what to do the next time he is attacked. I suggested he stop being so passive. I encouraged him to look his attacker in the eye, stay calm, focused, and refuse to give in to his assailant's outrageous demands...and to resolve, if necessary, to fight him as if his life depended upon it.

Not every police officer would agree with my suggestions. But this crime, as common as it is, is also unique. The victim is another individual in network marketing. The criminal is fear. The crime is theft... of dreams and

131

courage. The aftermath leaves many victims paralyzed and unable to grow their businesses. And the loss of productivity and revenue to individuals, families, corporations, and the general economy is inestimable. This thief must be faced, fought, and conquered.

> *"...involvement is a tangible demonstration of their courageous desire to change their lives."*

I have seen some of the most prodigiously gifted people in the world do little with their lives. Not because they are lazy, unmotivated, or without ambition. Not because they lack a dream or the will to work. But because fear has a choke-hold on them that renders them immobile. In network marketing, fear is the invisible cause for lack of productivity and success. The sensation of fear obscures vision, changes goals, and shifts priorities.

Here is a common example. Ed came into his network marketing business with a clear vision of what he wanted to accomplish and earn. He was motivated, excited, liked people, and had a wonderful work ethic. He made his list of people to call, bought his materials, went to training, planned his schedule, etc. On paper, he looked like he should have phenomenal success in network marketing.

Unfortunately for Ed, the cassette tapes that played in his mind told him that he was not competent enough to speak with "the professionals" or small business owners in his little community. This erroneous belief created the sensation of anxiety every time Ed was ready to speak with one of the people who intimidated him. Over time, Ed fell into a pattern. In his mind he would honestly plan and intend to speak with the people who threatened him. He would write down to whom he would speak, when to speak with them, and rehearse what he was going to say. From a distance, in his mind's eye, it all went beautifully. He was bold, articulate, and successful. He could easily envision his business growing.

But when the time arrived to interact with these people, Ed's imagined confidence vanished. In the moment of truth, when it was time to actually speak to people who intimidated him, Ed abruptly changed course. His vision of success was gone. His dream seemed laughable. The business he was excited about now seemed silly. And the thought that anyone would listen and respond to him felt like the most foolish thing he had ever imagined.

In a millisecond Ed changed his priorities. His big dreams, long-term goals, future plans, and good intentions were all traded for one simple but immediate goal: get rid of the fear. He wanted the anxiety to be gone. Now! And in that anxious moment he did not care what it would cost him in the future - as long as he could have peace in the present. He traded very real and achievable future success and accomplishment for the illusion of calm in the immediate moment. In the end, he will realize he made a terrible trade. It was a huge mistake. But at the moment of decision it felt like the bargain of a lifetime. Because in that moment of discomfort, all he wanted was relief from anxiety.

This same mistake is repeated by thousands of people in network marketing every day. When they begin to feel anxious and out of their comfort zones, they unconsciously shift their goals. They temporarily suspend the pursuit of their dreams and the growth of their businesses. For the moment, they simply want to avoid that which causes them discomfort. Initially, this little choice seems small, innocuous, and inconsequential. What they don't realize is that they are forming or reinforcing habits that make avoidance of discomfort a life style. For the future, this only makes the habit of avoidance stronger and the fear bigger.

> "You will face the fear of doing this business or you will face the fear of not doing this business."

Ed was stuck in this pattern of creating big dreams at night and trading them for imagined calm by day. I knew the patterns Ed was falling into. I knew the strangle hold of his erroneous beliefs and their concomitant feelings of anxiety. To break the power of this pattern I injected some cold reality into Ed's world. (I could say this because Ed knew that I cared about him and that I believed in him more than he believed in himself.) I simply told him point blank: "Ed, I know you are frightened and feel too intimidated to talk to some people. But let me tell you something. *"You will either face the fear of doing network marketing or you will face the fear of NOT doing network marketing. The choice is yours."*

I then challenged him to look at the cost/benefit analysis of this behavior. What are the immediate benefits of avoiding his fears and what are the costs? Here are some of the things we discussed:

BENEFITS OF AVOIDING FEAR

1. Avoidance seems to make the fear diminish.

2. It allows me to experience calm.

3. It allows me to avoid doing what I dislike.

4. It allows me to do something else that is more enjoyable.

5. It allows me to live within my comfort zone.

COSTS OF AVOIDING FEAR

1. Continued avoidance only makes my fear stronger.

2. Avoidance increases my stress and only camouflages my anxiety.

3. Avoidance prevents the growth of my business.

4. Avoidance prevents the growth of me as a person.

5. Avoidance sabotages my confidence.

6. Avoiding little fears today will create very real and large fears in the future.

7. Avoidance will cost me my dream.

8. Avoidance will keep me right where I am financially.

9. The little things I avoid today will be the big regrets of my future.

10. Trading years and years of future freedom to avoid brief moments of discomfort is a horrific life and business decision.

A cost/benefit analysis of avoiding fear. Notice that the costs are real, significant, and long term. The benefits are mostly imagined or temporary.

135

Fortunately for Ed, this injection of reality got him back in the game. He realized that avoiding his fear was solving no problems and creating future ones. He began to face his fears, pushed through them, and finally conquered them.

There are still aspects of growing his business that he does not particularly enjoy, but he does not let an unpleasant moment rob him of his dream or the pursuit of his goals. He acknowledges his feelings without allowing them to be the final arbitrator of his life choices. As a result he is growing more than a successful business. He is growing as a person. It is the ultimate win - win situation. And Ed knows that this is a whole lot more gratifying than the alternative he almost got duped into buying.

WHAT ABOUT YOU?

Are you ready to chase your dream and grow your business? Then you will have to face your fears. You will have to step out of your comfort zone and do things that are new, different, and uncomfortable. There is no way to avoid this because you have to grow as a person if you are going to grow a successful business.

Understandably, many people would like to grow a phenomenally successful business without ever getting out of their comfort zones. They want great success with no stress. They want great achievement with no anxiety. They want great rewards with no risk or hard work. It is understandably attractive. Unfortunately it is not possible. It is like trying to go swimming without having to get into the water. You cannot do one without the other.

As you envision growing your business, what are some of the things that are least comfortable for you? What are you afraid of? What will you be tempted to avoid, delay, or ignore? What are the action points that you will never get around to even though you know they are important?

What skills or actions are part of growing a business that tempt you to disqualify yourself from involvement?

You know yourself well enough to be able to identify your pockets of self-doubt. You already know where you will drag your feet. You can already identify your areas of internal resistance. You might even know the excuses and reasons you will give to yourself for avoiding action in these areas.

You can readily identify the activities that cause you discomfort because you are the expert in knowing yourself. You have been living with yourself and the things that you like to avoid for a long time.

Now take a moment and write down those skills or activities that cause you discomfort. This is your first step in managing your fear rather then letting your fear manage you. Your list is unique to you. But there are some common areas of discomfort that many people share. Some of these are: fear of speaking, rejection, being laughed at or misunderstood, not knowing how to answer questions, not being taken seriously, etc. Whatever yours are, list them below.

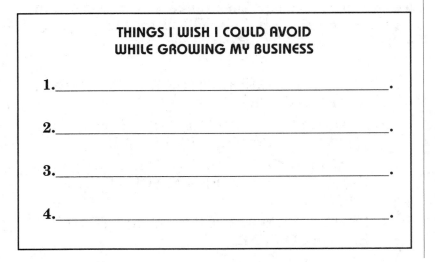

**THINGS I WISH I COULD AVOID
WHILE GROWING MY BUSINESS**

1._____.

2._____.

3._____.

4._____.

After making your list ask yourself these questions. How long have I been living with this area of discomfort? What price have I already paid to keep avoiding it? What price will I pay in the future if I keep avoiding it? Is the price too high? What will I commit to do for myself and my business regardless of the initial discomfort?

When people allow fear to control their lives, they have given their power away. They are allowing fear to be their designated drivers. And it is a worthless designated driver. At best, it will only drive them in circles. In the end they will realize that fear took them nowhere and kept them in the very place they were attempting to leave.

WOULD YOU LIKE THE CAR KEYS?

So where do you want to go from here? The choice and the power are yours. If you are in, or about to join a network marketing company, I suggest that you want to be the designated driver of your life and future. I commend you for that. Your involvement suggests that your life is at a crossroads. You are at the intersection of OLD HABITS and NEW OPPORTUNITY. My hope is that you will make a right turn onto the avenue of New Opportunity. As you progress down the road I further hope that you will:

1. ALLOW YOURSELF TO BE THE DESIGNATED DRIVER.

2. ZEALOUSLY GUARD THE CASSETTE TAPES THAT YOU ALLOW TO BE PLAYED.

3. GLADLY ACCEPT THE FACT THAT YOUR FINANCES AND FUTURE ARE YOUR RESPONSIBILITY.

4. DON'T GIVE YOUR POWER AWAY - TO OTHERS OR TO FEAR.

5. AS YOU DRIVE, REMEMBER THAT THIS IS "*1GR8DAY*".

6. *XPT2WN*

7. THIS IS <u>YOUR</u> MOMENT IN TIME. GRAB THE KEYS. DRIVE YOUR BUSINESS. HEAD FOR THE WINNERS' CIRCLE. YOU BELONG THERE.

Part Three:

THE POWER OF LEADERSHIP IN NETWORK MARKETING

CHAPTER NINE

LEADERSHIP IN A VOLUNTEER ARMY

Look at any network marketing company, and you will inevitably see an array of titles and positions available to any rep who works hard and effectively. Most people who have been around a company for a while can tell you exactly what is necessary to acquire their next title or promotion. This is appropriate because the most important position for representatives is the *next one* they can attain. Focusing on the next promotion as a goal is what gives them direction in the daily development of their businesses.

But what do the titles and positions mean? Do they signify anything? Do they have any substantive meaning? Or do they just indicate the pecking order or the relative amount of income received by holders of those titles and positions?

My belief is that the various titles used in network marketing companies are much more important than just suggesting the relative success someone has achieved; they are not meaningless. They are leadership titles.

But there are questions which require answers: What does it mean to be a leader? What is the essence of leadership? How does one develop as a leader? How does one exercise leadership in a network marketing company where everyone is an independent rep? These questions become increasingly important as a team grows because the people on the team are looking for some form of leadership or direction from us.

Network Marketing Requires the Highest Form of Leadership

One of the most positive and unique aspects of network marketing is the way leadership is exercised. In reality, network marketing requires a higher level of true leadership than is needed in traditional places of employment. There is no room for the negative forms of leadership commonly manifested in the traditional work setting. Fear, shame, guilt, or intimidation cannot be used as substitutes for genuine leadership. This is what is so appealing to people involved with the industry. It is also what makes leadership of a growing team so wonderfully challenging.

In network marketing no formal lines of authority exist over the people on our teams. They do not work "for us". We cannot fire them, nor can we withhold their salaries, promotions, or bonuses. We cannot dictate when, where, or how people on our teams will work. We have no "golden handcuffs" to keep them on-task. Since we have no formal authority over these people, we cannot make them do anything! They are volunteers. They can go A.W.O.L (absent without leave) anytime they want to. And there is nothing we can do about it! We are leaders in a volunteer army. As such, it requires the finest and highest form of leadership.

What Does It Mean to Be a Leader?

Let's look at some standard descriptions of leadership I often use:

1. *A leader is someone who knows where he / she is going and is able to motivate others to come along with him / her.*
2. *A leader is able to answer three questions: <u>Where</u> are we going? <u>How</u> are we going to get there? <u>Why</u> are we doing it this way?*
3. *Leadership is showing someone the way and then stepping out of the way.*
4. *Leadership is providing vision, skill, and motivation.*
5. *Leadership by title or position is different from leadership by influence.*

Leadership can be defined in numerous ways. But in the world of network marketing, there are some qualities of leadership that are imperative to understand, no matter what particular definition of leadership you prefer. Some of these qualities include modeling to others, serving them, and being patient with them.

LEADERSHIP IS MODELING TO OTHERS

If you could assemble your ideal network marketing team, what are some of the common characteristics you would like to see exhibited by its members? What behaviors or habits would these people have? What would they do to positively impact the growth of their businesses? What would they model to others? For openers, look at the following list:

- self-starter
- hard worker
- works well with others
- visionary/entrepreneur
- not easily discouraged
- stays positive and optimistic
- enthusiastic and motivated
- adequate product knowledge
- sets and keeps daily/weekly goals
- doesn't take a "no" personally
- is in the business for the long haul

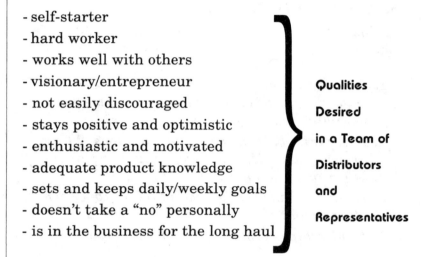

Qualities Desired in a Team of Distributors and Representatives

Up Close and Personal

Now let's bring this list "up close and personal." As people observe us growing our businesses, what do they see us model? Whether we like it or not, our teams will do what we do. They will see what we do and follow our lead. They will draft off of us. The new people who join our teams will look to us to get their bearings. They will observe what we do and conclude that this is the way business is conducted in this organization. This is why it is important to understand that *a vital dimension of effective leadership is modeling.*

If new people are going to be on time for our meetings, they need to see us there on time. If they are going to take our events seriously, they need to see us take them seriously. Too often, I have seen leaders who have been around their network marketing businesses for a while act as if they are too busy and too important to sit through the business presentation one more time. They may sit in the back of the room (or leave the room altogether) so they can do "more important things." When they do this, they make a huge mistake. While they believe it shows others how busy and important they are, they are greatly mistaken. What it suggests is that they no longer get excited about their business. The place for leaders is in the meeting, towards the front, forcing themselves to remain focused, energized, and animated about the same business opportunity they have seen, heard, or given countless times. They are modeling to others that they still get excited about their business.

If we want people to host in-home meetings, are we also hosting them? If we want our teams to share their businesses with others, are they seeing us do it too? If we want our teams to utilize technology (a weekly conference call, voice mail system, e-mail, videoconferencing, fax on demand, etc.), are we good examples? If we want them to have adequate products to grow their businesses, do they see us utilizing these supplies? If we want our people to regularly attend meetings and conventions, do they see us do the same? If we want them to be available to others, promptly return phone calls and assist new reps, do they see us model these actions?

The concept of modeling reminds us that there is a direct correlation between what leaders *do* and what gets *duplicated* on their teams. That is why there is truth to the leadership adage, "If you want your people to bleed, then you need to hemorrhage!" People who are new to network marketing will look to their upline to set the pace, show the way, and model the attitude, vigor, and manner in which the business is built and a team developed.

An ironic aspect of modeling is what the others on our team will do. They may be slow to duplicate the numerous things we do well, but they will quickly identify and replicate habits that are less than helpful in business development. As you think through the ideal qualities and habits you would like to see represented on your team, be sure you are modeling them to the best of your ability. This is both the privilege and responsibility of leadership.

LEADERSHIP IS SERVING OTHERS

Positions and leadership titles can sound impressive. From a distance, leadership appears glamorous. It looks like it is fun and full of endless accolades and privileges. Those in positions of significant leadership seem to be admired by many and disliked by few. Their leadership positions suggest prestige and honor. Appropriately, these often accompany a leadership role. To outsiders, leadership may appear as an exceptionally and endlessly enjoyable lifestyle. When examined more closely, there are other dimensions of leadership that are less appealing.

Those who are enjoying the fulfilling aspects of leadership have been paying their dues in other areas of leadership that are anything but enviable. Long before you see an individual enjoying the fruits of leadership in public, he or she has earned the right of public praise or personal success in private. They have paid their dues in a thousand ways for a thousand days. They did what others weren't willing to do. Now they enjoy things that others do not.

The Heart Of Leadership

What is the heart of leadership? At its core, it is much less glamorous than you might think. Leadership is a fancy word for head servant. It means you get to be the head waiter, chief, cook, and bottle washer. Those who have attained it know that leadership means long days, hard work, and more responsibility. They know that:

LEADERSHIP IS:

- *The privilege of working while others sleep.*
- *The privilege of reading or researching while others rest.*
- *The privilege of spending time driving their businesses while others drive a golf ball.*
- *The privilege of working hard in their businesses to make their dreams become reality while others work hard to block out the reality that they have no dreams.*
- *The privilege of praying for wisdom while others are out playing with no worries.*
- *The privilege of routinely giving themselves to their teams while others give themselves to television.*
- *The privilege of ignoring fatigue and focusing on daily goals while others capitulate to fatigue and forget their daily goals.*
- *The privilege of being servants to their teams and their own life goals, while others have no goals or teams to which to give themselves.*
- *The privilege of delayed gratification. Doing what they may not feel like doing today so they can do, have, and become what they want in the future. Meanwhile, nonleaders do all the little and insignificant things they want to do today at the expense of all the big and significant things they wish for in the future.*

The "Not So Glamorous" Side of Leadership

Leaders, in reality, are people who are yielded. They have yielded themselves to their dreams, goals, and teams. They live each day in light of these. Ironically, giving themselves over to these is what gives them strength and focus. It is what makes them tough.

While learning to be tough on themselves, true leaders also understand the art of working with others. Leadership, especially in network marketing, requires that we be patient, positive, and honest with others. Knowing how and when to use each of these is one of the most important dimensions of effective leadership.

AS A LEADER, BE PATIENT WITH REPS

As leaders begin to comprehend the power of network marketing and exponential growth, they will increasingly long for a team of motivated self-starters. They will start to sense what it could mean to have tens, then hundreds, then thousands of people on a team working several hours per week.

They begin to see that on their own they cannot work much more than fifty hours per week, or two hundred hours per month in their businesses. (50 hours per week x 4 weeks = 200 hours) Additionally, they know that if they do work this many hours they will have little time left over to enjoy the fruit of their labor. But, if they had five hundred reps on a team who, on average, worked only five hours per week, then the total number of hours invested in the business would jump to 10,000 collective human hours per month! (500 people x 5 hours x 4 weeks) And no one would feel overworked!

As leaders experience what it is to leverage time while creating residual income, they will have new appreciation for those individuals on their team who set goals, stay focused, and work consistently. Simultaneously, they will be tempted to become frustrated or impatient with others on their teams who seem to be doing very little. They will want these people to be more excited, motivated, active, and productive. They will begin to say things like, "I just wish I could find people who would be willing to work this business as hard as I am. I wish I could find someone like me!"

This is understandable because somewhere along the way, anyone who is serious about building a business will discover one of the great truths about life in the world of network marketing:

The best thing about this business is also the worst thing about this business!

Our ability to grow a team, develop residual income, and create wealth is completely contingent upon the efforts of others. Other like-minded entrepreneurs are needed. As leaders, we need to be patient while we find or develop them.

To develop patience with your reps, keep in mind:

1. The private lives of new reps do not stop because they have joined your team and company.
2. Signing up on paper to be a rep is not the same thing as signing up with heart, mind, or will.

Life Doesn't Stop Because Someone Joined Your Team

In most cases, people who join your team had a full schedule before they got involved with your business. They were already busy. Trying to rearrange the rhythm and schedule of life is not easy. Be patient while they discover how to fit their new businesses into their daily routines.

It is easy to tell people that the beauty of network marketing is that they can work their business part-time and at their convenience. Then, after they join your team, you'll secretly wish they were immediately working their own businesses on a nearly full-time basis! We want them to have the same passion, conviction, and zeal that we have. No matter how committed they are to growing their businesses, remember they still have relationships to attend to, jobs to go to, bills to pay, errands to run, etc.

> *"If you want your people to bleed then you need to hemorrhage!"*

Signing Up on Paper....

Leaders also need to remember that signing an application to be a rep is not the same thing as signing up with heart, mind, and will. These are often two separate events. Many people sign up to join a network marketing company because they *briefly saw* the power and potential of this industry via some form of business presentation. However, not long after signing up, the excitement and willingness to work begin to erode. Old tapes begin to play in their minds; old beliefs prompt them to return to the worlds they know. They go back to their "comfort zones" and begin to doubt the very opportunity that got them so animated when they signed up.

This "battle of belief" is a common occurrence for anyone starting any new endeavor. For many people in network marketing, the battle is lost rather than won. This is why the first hours, days, and weeks in the business are so critical. Like a new-born baby, new reps may have arrived, but they are a long way from being self-sufficient. Support, assistance, and direction are needed from the upline while their beliefs are taking shape.

Many reps enter their businesses with great excitement and a modest amount of conviction or belief. This is an acceptable starting point. Eventually, however, belief and conviction must become the bedrock foundation for a business to grow. These characteristics must also become a source of excitement because they provide staying power and resilience. While belief and conviction are being developed, leaders must be patient; they know new reps are still sorting out their beliefs. Even if the new reps are not consciously aware of it, they are developing answers to the following questions:

- *What do I believe about the company I have affiliated with?*

- *What do I believe about the products/services we represent?*

- *What do I believe about network marketing as a business/marketing strategy?*

- *What will others believe about this industry and the company and products I represent?*

- *What do I believe about the compensation potential in this endeavor?*

- *Do I believe someone could succeed in this company if they worked hard, consistently, and did not quit?*

- *Do I believe that I will work this business hard, consistently, and not quit?*
- *Do I believe I can succeed in this business?*
- *Do I believe I will succeed in this business?*
- *Do I believe in myself?*

These progressive levels of belief must be developed in order for individuals to succeed in network marketing. While these beliefs are being developed, leaders need to be patient with each new team member. (Note that the most important and the most personal beliefs are at the end of the process.)

What is it that enables some people to work, in a seemingly effortless manner, all the way through these questions which have to be faced in any significant endeavor? What makes some people in network marketing capable of working hard, staying focused, and growing their businesses while others just fade away? There are numerous factors that can influence an individual's ability to stay on-task. (The clarity of their dreams, their levels of discipline, their ego strengths, the levels of support they receive from their team, etc.) But for now, let's look at characteristics that are common to everyone in a network marketing business for the long term. Understanding these characteristics helps leaders be patient with their reps.

LEADERS UNDERSTAND "THE THREE FUELS"

Imagine your involvement with a network marketing company as a running race. Now, picture the runners gaining strength from three different fuel sources: enthusiasm, commitment, and conviction. Each of these fuel sources are very important, and they each serve a different function.

ENTHUSIASM: Fuel #1

COMMITMENT: Fuel #2

CONVICTION: Fuel #3

Enthusiasm is a good fuel for brief sprints. Commitment is a good fuel for running intermediate races. Conviction is the only fuel that sustains people for a marathon.

Enthusiasm: Fuel #1

The process of starting in network marketing is the same for many individuals. They hear about the business, sense the financial potential, and imagine how success in this business could change their lives. Together, these fuel enthusiasm. As a result, the new reps are focused and fired up. With enthusiasm as their only fuel source they come out of the starting blocks at full sprint. Or, as Bob Torsey kids, they start out "I.O.F." (ignorance on fire!) The race looks so simple they are sure it cannot be much more than a 100-meter race. At the finish line they see opportunity, potential, and wealth.

But somewhere during the race it begins to dawn on new reps that this race is not a 100-meter sprint. It is not even an 800- or 1000-meter race. It is a marathon. And this emerging realization, that growing a large network marketing business is not a little sprint or "just a walk in the park," brings reps to the first major point of decision. How will they respond to this reality? And what should they do now that their fuel supply of enthusiasm is beginning to run low?

At this point many reps stop for a moment to rest, and they are never seen on the track again. What happened? They had no other fuel supply to draw on to keep them going. So when their enthusiasm was gone, so were they.

155

One of the most remarkable sprints I remember was that of an individual who came to a meeting as an avowed skeptic. When the meeting was over, he was the first one to pull out his check book and sign up. He raced out of the meeting, sure he didn't need to stick around for any training and instruction. He went home to become wealthy in a single evening. He got on the phone I.O.F. (ignorance on fire!) and promptly got rejected by his sister. With that he phoned the meeting host to say he was done with his new business. I just rolled with laughter. This guy couldn't sprint 20 meters before he hit the wall! He didn't last two hours in the business. What happened? He made the common mistake of thinking he could create serious wealth without serious work. He discovered it takes more than enthusiasm to be a winner in network marketing. When the fuel supply ran out, so did he.

How do the other two fuels, commitment and conviction, help sustain someone as a long distance runner? The first will make you an intermediate distance runner, and the second will make you a marathon runner.

The Tail Wagging the Dog

Many reps join a network marketing company and are filled with enthusiasm. There are legitimate reasons for them to be very enthusiastic. But too many reps begin their businesses high on enthusiasm and low on commitment and conviction. When their enthusiasm and emotional excitement begin to diminish, they have no back-up systems. They have nothing else to draw upon. So they pace their work in their businesses based on their emotions and feelings. If they are *feeling* motivated or inspired, they may do something. But they will not do anything without the only fuel supply they know... enthusiasm.

> **"Leaders did what others weren't willing to do. Now they enjoy things that others do not."**

When our feelings and emotions become the primary basis for behavioral decisions, we are at risk. At this point, our feelings direct us to the path of least resistance and toward what feels most comfortable *in the present moment*. When this happens, the tail is wagging the dog. Thoughtful, purposeful living is held captive to the whims of momentary desire.

When enthusiasm is diminishing, reps need something else to draw upon to keep them going. Just as some trucks come equipped with two fuel tanks so that a driver can switch tanks when one gets low, reps need another fuel tank to switch to when their fuel supply of enthusiasm is running dry. The next fuel tank to switch to is commitment.

Commitment: Fuel #2

Commitment runs on more than just feelings or emotions. It brings the force of the will and the mind into the decision process. When reps approach their businesses with commitment, they have a sense of purpose and focus. They know why they want to develop their businesses, what they want out of them, and they have a more long-term view. They see beyond their immediate feelings. With a strong commitment they sustain long-term focus. They can override or ignore emotions and feelings that encourage them to quit, coast, or back off for a while. This ability of commitment to "pull rank" over emotions that cry out for immediate comfort is a profoundly significant component of maturity in life. In network marketing, it provides the fuel to keep going when people begin to experience the reality that growing their businesses is neither a sprint nor a fun little jog.

There will be stretches, however, when even commitment is sorely tested in the race to build a large team and business, just as any other major achievement in life will test us to the breaking point. It is at this point of decision that we will either begin to slow down, or we will switch fuel tanks and finally be fueled by conviction. It is this superior fuel supply that allows people to settle in for the marathon of network marketing. Ironically, when reps tap into conviction, there is a major replenishing of both enthusiasm and commitment.

Conviction: Fuel #3

What is conviction? It is unflinching belief. It is an attitude. A state of mind. It is unshakable faith. It is internal confidence. It is certitude. It is the resolute knowledge that "my business will work for me if I will work my business!" It is what gives reps undaunted courage and tenacity when they "hit the wall" in the network marketing marathon. It keeps them going when fatigue, slow growth, or doubt tempt them to quit dreaming, stop expecting, and cease working. Conviction is the one common characteristic of every individual with staying power in network marketing.

How is conviction in a network marketing business developed? Internal conviction is often developed by osmosis. It is assimilated from time spent with other people who have it. That is why association is such a critical success component. Reps become like those with whom they associate. When reps put themselves in a position to watch, listen, interact with, and learn from leaders with conviction, this characteristic begins to grow within them as well.

The growth of conviction is also a function of time, experience, and success. If reps give their businesses enough time and do what is necessary to learn how to develop them effectively, success will come. And success

> *"Conviction is the one common characteristic of every individual with staying power in network marketing."*

has a unique capacity to recreate itself. Success breeds further success. Like yeast in a bread dough, success keeps growing when it's in the proper environment.

As Your Team Grows...

If you have a new participant in network marketing on your team, give him or her time to develop conviction. It is fine to start with enthusiasm and commitment. They are wonderful qualities. I pity people who go through life without them. But as a rep consistently grows a business, you will discover that their level of conviction has been quietly growing as well.

In conjunction with the growth of your business and your conviction, your team will grow. As it does, be patient with others while they learn to tap into the fuel of conviction. Remember that signing up on paper to join your business is not the same thing as signing up with their heart, mind, and soul. These are usually separate events. Your reps' beliefs are still developing. In the meantime, model to them your own enthusiasm and commitment. Let them sense your growing conviction. Let the power of association with you be what energizes them to keep believing, keep expecting, and keep working.

As you lead your growing team, keep in mind that leadership is just a fancy word for "servant." You get to be the head waiter, the one who works the hardest, gives the most, and sets the pace. After accepting the responsibility of leadership, you will one day know its flip side...the benefits of leadership.

This point was driven home to me recently while my wife and I were having lunch with Bob and Liz McEwen. Bob is a former Member of Congress who, along with his wife, now works full-time in one of the flagship network marketing companies. They both understand a great deal about the nature of leadership. While relaxing over lunch, I asked them how leadership was modeled to them in their organization. They mentioned that their sponsor is one of the most successful people in the history of network marketing and also one of the wealthiest people in America. When I asked them to explain the phenomenal success of this individual, Liz simply replied, "He could be a king. But all he wants to be is a king-maker."

Do you want to grow a large successful organization? Follow this leader's example. Don't try to be a king or a queen. Instead, be a king- and queen-maker. The rest will take care of itself. Remember, leadership is just a fancy word for servant.

CHAPTER TEN

LEADERSHIP: HELPING OTHERS BE THEIR BEST

Network marketing is not just about creating significant income. The dignity and richness of this industry often go unnoticed as we work at making a difference in what our reps believe about themselves, what they can become, and what they can do. While there are numerous aspects of leadership that people find attractive, this one, for me, stands head and shoulders above all others.

Many people like the thought of achieving leadership titles or positions. Even more, they like the thought of attaining leadership qualities. But others, even those already in leadership positions, sometimes have little concept of what a leader is actually supposed to do. This becomes particularly true when they move beyond their daily tasks toward the art of working with those whom they have the honor of leading. Some may be better at tending to things than to people. While getting things done and being productive are vital components of success, they are not the entire story when it comes to leadership.

Skilled leaders know what to do with the people they are leading. They know the art and science of working with others. In network marketing, there are several things we need to keep in mind as leaders if we are going to grow large businesses and teams. Among the most important leadership attributes are believing in people—even more than they believe in themselves, and knowing how to be honest with people—even when we have difficult things to say.

BELIEVE IN THEM MORE THAN THEY BELIEVE IN THEMSELVES

By the time we are adults, all of us have spoken more words than we can count. Curiously, even though we speak every day, most of us have never fully comprehended the power of language to transform a life or simply to make someone's day a little brighter. Leaders must understand the power of genuine encouragement.

There are countless people in network marketing (as well as in the political and corporate worlds) who are eminently successful for one reason: someone believed in them more than they believed in themselves. The power of someone else's believing in them gave them just enough gumption to get up and get going. It gave them just enough energy to pursue their dreams, which in turn became the reality that changed their lives.

Avoid Shame-based Leadership

When individuals on your team are not doing as much as you would like them to, be careful not to resort to shame-based leadership. Many leaders use guilt and shame to try to motivate others. This is a common but very unsophisticated form of leadership. The essence of leadership is building people up, not breaking them down. This is particularly important in network marketing because reps do not have to stick around and take abuse. Many of them already have others in their work or home environments who remind them every day that they are not measuring up. If we begin to sound like just one more person telling them they are basically a disappointment and a failure, they will soon be gone. They are looking for a positive and motivating reference group. As leaders, if we provide this, we might unleash a wellspring of talent, energy, and focus that has heretofore been untapped.

See What They Have and Share What You See

Study those with whom you have the privilege of working. What traits, talents, or qualities do you see in them that will be assets to their future success? (For example, notice if they excel at working with people or details. Are they self-starters? Are they good at follow-through, creativity, being a team player, full of enthusiasm or laughter, well received by others?) As a leader, study their strengths. See what they have and then share what you see. Don't let your positive observations go unexpressed. There is a reason Mark Twain commented that he could run for thirty days on the strength of one compliment. He understood that words of legitimate *encouragement* allow people to live in a state of courage.

Knowing how to genuinely encourage others does not preclude us as leaders from occasionally sharing negative news. In reality, I have found that people are much more receptive to believing the kind things I have to say to them when they are just as confident that I will also share the difficult things.

AS A LEADER, LEARN TO BE HONEST WITH OTHERS

One of the things I most enjoy about network marketing is the quality of people the industry attracts. For the most part, they are a wonderful group of people: friendly, courteous, outgoing, excited about the possibilities life holds, and easy to be with. For many of these people, their greatest strength is the easy and friendly manner in which they relate to others. This is a tremendous quality. But when taken to an extreme, it can be a liability in the area of leadership because there are moments when leaders need to say some hard things that may be painful to hear. They need to be the messengers of news that is neither fun to deliver nor to receive. But this is a necessary part of leadership.

However, in many network marketing groups the atmosphere is one that suggests everyone is welcome, that they can grow their businesses as they see fit, and they are free to do as they please. Like the Outback Steakhouse slogan, the motto seems to be "no rules, just right." In a way, this is true, since we have no formal authority over anyone. On the other hand, as individuals "pay their dues" over the years and develop their businesses, their attitudes begin to change. They begin to take their businesses much more seriously. Consequently, they begin to take leadership and speaking honestly with others more seriously as well.

Initially, many leaders try to lead their growing organization while avoiding the need to be honest with others. It is a nice wish but it isn't possible. Be careful not to confuse being friendly or popular with leadership; they are not always the same thing. *If your goal is to be liked by everyone, it will be difficult to lead anyone.*

Over time, many leaders learn the value of honesty the hard way. Out of exasperation, frustration, or exhaustion, they finally begin to speak honestly with others who are ineffective in growing their businesses. Unfortunately, these leaders do this only as a last resort.

In their beginning role as leaders, they attempt to endlessly "flex" with people in their organization. They put on a game face and act as though another person's

> *"They are successful for one reason: someone believed in them more than they believed in themselves."*

lack of productivity or poor attitude are not problems. These leaders may attempt to ignore things, look the other way, and swallow their frustration. For example, most veterans of network marketing know what it is to fly, or drive, hundreds of miles to a meeting that was poorly promoted. They arrive only to find that there are no new guests. And many of the people who are already in their business are not even there. In order to keep up the morale of their team, they conceal their frustration. They act as if all of the time, money, and energy they invested to get to the meeting don't matter.

Eventually, many of these reps discover they are getting a massive case of "emotional indigestion." As leaders, they are beginning to feel more like suckers than servants. It begins to occur to them that their time and efforts are neither respected nor taken seriously by those they are attempting to help. They finally realize that while they need to be available *to* others, they have no desire to be taken advantage of *by* others. It dawns on them that their methods are not working. Instead of developing a team of independent reps, they are getting a team of DEPENDENT people who are neither growing as a team nor as leaders.

This can be a very important and helpful experience for most reps. Handled properly, it will not make them angry or bitter. Instead, it will make them tougher, stronger, more forceful and direct. It sets them free to be candid with those whom they are attempting to lead. They begin to be more honest, establish boundaries, and clarify expectations.

Speaking the Truth

In true leadership, the right to say difficult things to another person does not come because one has a formal leadership title. The right to say hard things to someone comes from having *earned the right* to say hard things. This right comes *after* others know we care about them, after they know we believe in them and that we want to set them up for a win in their businesses. When they finally understand we are committed to their well being, then we have the right to speak. (This knowledge also disposes reps to be much more willing to listen.)

Additionally, knowing *what* to say, *how* to say it, and *when* to say it is a vital aspect of mature leadership. Maybe that is why King David wrote, "A wise man chooses his speech judiciously and adds much persuasiveness to his lips." He understood the importance of word selection, especially when we have difficult things to say to someone.

The Two Parts of Honesty: Content and Context

There are two parts to honesty that are often overlooked. They are *content* and *context*. The first part deals with what we say. The second deals with the manner in which we say it.

Many people in network marketing get one part right but not the other. Some people are very good at delivering the truth. That is, they have no problem saying hard-to-hear things to people. But they do it with no regard for the impact. Their style may be harsh, uncaring, and poorly timed. There is no love. Just information. This imbalance makes these leaders much less effective than they would be if they had learned to share what they have to say in a softer and wiser style.

On the other hand, there are countless network marketing leaders who err on the other side of speaking the truth. They are very good at the contextual side of leadership. They are good at liking others and creating a pleasant context for work. They want to encourage others. However, they only want to share nice, positive thoughts or feelings with others. They don't want to hurt anyone else's feelings, and they want everyone to be happy. So they avoid saying anything that might upset the recipient. They never say anything negative, even when it is true. As a result, many of the people they lead keep endlessly repeating the same mistakes because no one told them what they needed to hear. They were only told what they wanted to hear. In the end, this is very expensive for everyone.

So How Do You Do This?

While learning to be honest with others on your team, keep a few things in mind. Be sure you have modeled the business to them correctly. Be certain you have been appropriately patient and positive. Remember, sharing negative news with someone is something we must do sparingly and with great care and respect.

When I am working with someone to whom I must give negative news (and it doesn't matter if it is someone on my network marketing team, a corporate leader, or a Member of Congress - the format is always about the same.) I will say something like the following:

> "John, do you know that I care about you?"
>
> "Yes, Tom. I don't doubt that."
>
> "Do you know that I am committed to you?"
>
> "Yeah, Tom. I know that."
>
> "Do you know that I want you to win as much as you want to win in this business?"
>
> "I believe that, Tom."
>
> "I'm glad you know these things because today I am going to hit you right between the eyes. If you are serious about wanting to be a winner you need to pay attention to...."

What am I doing in the above dialogue? I am speaking the truth in love. I am balancing content and context. In effect, I am putting one of my arms around them to hold them while I punch them in the nose with the other. It is the depth of my caring that gives them the strength to handle the force of my message.

As your team and your leadership comfort grow, you will periodically have to say something similar to those whom you serve. You might find the following questions and comments useful as you become more careful about the expenditure of your time:

> " (Name of person), do you know that I care about you?"

"Do you know that I believe in you? Maybe even more than you believe in yourself?"

"Do you know that I believe you have what it takes to be remarkably successful in our business?"

"Good. Here is something else I want you to know."

If you want to learn, I will teach you.

If you want to follow, I will lead you.

If you want to learn how to be a leader, I will set you up for leadership.

If you want to be "a player" on our team, I will help you. But if you just want to play, I don't have time for you.

If you want to develop a serious business, then I will make a serious commitment to you. But, if you just want to dabble, I will work with someone else.

Think it over. I know how much I believe in you and in our business. I just need to know where you want to fit in.

To some, the previous dialogue may sound too direct. In reality, when done properly, it is very freeing and establishes clear expectations and boundaries for everyone. It prevents those who are earnestly attempting to grow a business from spending endless hours with reps who have no intention of taking their business seriously. Also, it allows those who just want to dabble in their business to do so without feeling annoyed by their upline. Once we know where a rep stands, we know how to respectfully work with them or around them.

As individuals grow their businesses they will find themselves growing as leaders. While being fueled by enthusiasm, commitment, and conviction, their attitudes will appropriately mature in conjunction with their businesses. The following attitudes commonly develop among those who are serious about growing large and successful teams.

- They take their own business more seriously. It is still very enjoyable to them, but it is absolutely clear that their home-based business has, or is becoming, a very significant business venture. The more they see the magnitude of the opportunity, the less nonchalant they are about those who are just dabbling in their businesses.

- They begin to invest themselves in those who are teachable and who demonstrate a sincere desire to grow their businesses.

- They begin to have less patience and tolerance for people who are experts at only one thing: making excuses to explain why they haven't quite accomplished what they said they would.

- They become more careful about how, and to whom, they parcel out their time. As demand for their time increases, so does the value they place on it. They are not as quick to let other people waste it.

- They are appreciative of team players who "plug into the system" when they comprehend the invisible structure that creates wealth in network marketing.

  (Remember: wealth comes from depth. Depth comes from duplication. And duplication comes from having a system that is very simple.) Conversely, they are less appreciative of those who do not plug into the system. They know that until these people do plug into their system, any significant and ongoing success is highly improbable.

In some respects, leaders in network marketing are like athletic coaches. They develop trained eyes for studying people. They are looking for individuals with talent, teachability, and great hearts. They learn to ascertain where someone is on an imaginary continuum of involvement with their company. It might look like the following:

LEVELS OF COMMITMENT OR INVOLVEMENT

Level 1: **A Lark**- got involved on a whim; no intentions of seriously working their business; will try it and see if it is fun.

Level 2: **Just Dabbling**- no serious commitment or expectations; just playing with the business; "dinking around" with it.

Level 3: **A Hobby**- a form of entertainment; involved for fun, mild interest.

Level 4: **A Cute Little Business**- involved for fun with the idea that it might generate a "little extra spending money"; modest commitment and minimal expectations.

Level 5: **A Small, Home Based-Business**- moderate commitment with modest financial expectations; wonders if business might generate a few hundred dollars per month.

Level 6: **A Business** - increasing expectations and commitment; beginning to view a network

marketing business with moderate serious-
ness; realizes it could generate a few thousand dollars per month.

Level 7: **An Opportunity**- business is seen as having potential just like countless other "opportunities" that exist; if taken seriously,
it could create serious monthly revenue
over time.

Level 8: **MY Business**- significant increase in involvement, commitment, and expectations;
personal ownership has settled in.

Level 9: **MY Opportunity**- strong personal realization that network marketing is an invitation to change their finances and their
lives; high level of commitment and expectation.

Level 10: **MY BUSINESS, MY OPPORTUNITY,
MY MOMENT, MY VEHICLE**- a quan-
tum leap in insight, understanding, and
conviction; an attitude that suggests "I am
in this business and this business is in me";
it is "in the blood"; the magnitude of the
opportunity is sensed; the financial impli-
cations are obvious; the person is in the
business for the long haul and with full
commitment.

**This continuum demonstrates the different lev-
els of commitment people have to their businesses.
Leaders learn to detect the commitment level of
others, and they create environments to help move
their reps further along the continuum.**

As you consider this imaginary continuum, keep in
mind that the commitment level of people is not fixed. It

is fluid, and it can fluctuate up and down. For many people, belief and commitment levels increase over time just by association with others who are motivated and successful. Countless people have become involved with network marketing companies with almost no vision. They had little awareness of the vast potential of the business. However, as they consistently interacted with others who were excited, motivated, stayed focused, and consequently

> *"If your goal is to be liked by everyone it will be difficult to lead anyone."*

had success, they began to see their own vision, expectation, and commitment level increase. Today, their level of commitment is a ten. Now they patiently work with those who have much smaller levels of commitment because they know that some of these people will move up this continuum just as they did.

In assessing where others are on this continuum of commitment, be aware that people get involved with network marketing for three reasons: affiliation, recognition, and income. The motivation of those who get involved for affiliation is social and relational. They are content to meet new people, enjoy the group meetings or events, and have fun. The potential income is largely irrelevant to them. Similarly, those who get involved for recognition are not primarily motivated for financial gain. Their primary desire is to discover a place where their talents and contributions can be appreciated. They have a legitimate longing for their worth as an individual to be recognized and honored by others.

People who initially become involved with network marketing for affiliation and recognition can be a rich enhancement to any team. Those who join for affiliation can keep our businesses fun and enjoyable, and people who join for recognition can be excellent workers when they feel appreciated for their efforts. In either case, their levels of commitment can increase significantly over time as they begin to comprehend the revenue potential of their businesses. Be patient with these people; many of them, almost by accident, become top producers in their companies.

When Will I Begin to Lead?

I am often asked, "Tom, when will I begin to feel free to be a leader? When will I begin to step up to the plate and honestly start leading my team? When will I feel comfortable enough to tell people what they need to hear and not just what they want to hear?" These are great questions. My answer usually includes the following:

YOU WILL BEGIN TO TAKE LEADERSHIP SERIOUSLY:

1. *When YOU begin to take the industry of network marketing seriously.*

2. *When YOU begin to take YOUR business seriously.*

3. *When YOU begin to take your time seriously.*

4. *When YOU begin to take serving your team seriously.*

5. *When YOU begin to take yourself seriously.*

If you are new to network marketing or to leadership, don't let the idea of being a leader overwhelm you. Give yourself permission to grow into the leadership titles you acquire in the growth of your business. Remember, being a leader simply means that you get to be the head servant. You have the privilege of helping other people realize their goals and dreams by believing in them, encouraging them, and being honest with them. While focusing on helping others grow their businesses, many reps find they have become leaders themselves in the process.

In the desire to grow a network marketing business it is easy to inadvertently focus on the wrong things. I suggest a simple approach for staying properly focused, growing your business, and effectively leading others:

FOCUS ON YOUR REPS AND NOT ON THE REVENUE.

FOCUS ON YOUR PEOPLE AND NOT ON THE PROFIT.

FOCUS ON MAKING OTHERS SUCCESSFUL AND NOT ON THE MONEY.

FOCUS ON YOUR DOWNLINE AND NOT ON THE DIVIDENDS.

If you focus on the revenue and not on your reps, there will be no significant money to count. But, if you focus on building your downline and not on the dollars, in the end, you might end up with more money than you can count. There is a wonderful paradox to success in this industry: The only way to reach the top is by bending down and helping others.

"Leaders are like athletic coaches. They are looking for people with talent, teachability, and great hearts."

Lessons from Another Leader

Some time ago, my wife and I were having dinner with another couple. In the course of our conversation I discovered that the man had served on the personal staff of General Patton during his military career. Naturally I was curious and asked many of the standard questions about this remarkable leader. I inquired about his personality, what it was like to work with him each day, and about his pearl-handled six shooters. Then I asked if it was true that General Patton was as loved and respected by his men as history reports. Without a moment of hesitation he replied, "You bet!" Then I asked him to explain why this was the case. He thought quietly for a moment and then replied, "Because he loved his men, and he believed in what he was doing."

As you learn what it means to exercise leadership in a volunteer army, love the men and women on your team. Make a difference in what they believe about themselves, what they can become, and what they can do. And believe in what you are doing.

CHAPTER ELEVEN

LEADERSHIP: GIVING PEOPLE TRACKS TO RUN ON

Did you ever notice how towns and cities all across America try to have their own little claims to fame? Local citizens try to find something that makes their own community unique and allows them to be proud of it. In fact, they usually put up a welcome sign which will remind you of this uniqueness as you enter the city limits.

I grew up in Des Plaines, Illinois, and it too has its own point of distinction. Des Plaines is where the first McDonald's fast-food restaurant was opened. That particular McDonald's is still there and is now preserved as a museum. Not far from there is Hamburger University, where owners and managers of new McDonald's are trained.

I still recall when they put on their now-famous arches, that more than "one million" hamburgers had been sold. They used to change the sign in increments of one million. Finally, they changed the sign to say "millions and millions sold." Now the sign simply says "billions" sold. Several things about this amaze me. The people in my community were surrounded by one of the most extraordinary success stories in corporate history. We watched McDonald's grow from a simple idea and a single store into a worldwide economic force. Most of the local people were oblivious to what was happening with McDonald's. Some were admiringly aware of the company's success, but they never thought to get involved. Only a few were smart enough to see what was happening, admire the success, and get actively involved as an early franchise owner.

This same oversight is a daily occurrence in America and around the world. People are surrounded by high-quality network marketing companies. Most will be oblivious to the opportunities available. Some will admire what these companies are doing but they will never get actively involved. But a few will see the magnitude of an opportunity, seize it, and in the process change their futures and their lives as well.

View Each New Rep on Your Team As the Equivalent of a New Store Opening

We can learn a great deal from the phenomenal success and growth of McDonald's because in some ways our businesses are very similar. This becomes increasingly clear if you *view each new rep that comes into your business as the equivalent of a new store or franchise* that is opening. This vantage point makes you much more appreciative of every individual on your team and much more committed to training them for successful business operations.

While using McDonald's as an analogy of our network marketing business, let's briefly review my thesis of the invisible infrastructure that holds a successful network marketing business together. Then let's look and see if McDonald's understands and implements this same process.

WEALTH comes from *DEPTH*.

DEPTH comes from *DUPLICATION*.

DUPLICATION comes from having a *SYSTEM*.

A *SYSTEM* comes from keeping things very *SIMPLE*

As a business, has McDonald's generated phenomenal revenue or, to use our term, **wealth**? Absolutely. But how, beginning with a single store, did they do it? They did this by creating **depth** in their organization. One store at a time. Today that depth has resulted in their having tens of thousands of stores worldwide.

Why did McDonald's have such tremendous expansion success? From the very beginning, the company focused on **duplication**. Their goal was not to have the fanciest restaurant, serve the finest burger, or have the biggest menu. It was massive expansion through ongoing duplication. The repetitious opening of one store after another. (Maybe this is why Steve Schulz, who is a superb leader and earning a small fortune in his network marketing business, asks himself one business question when he goes to bed each night: "Can the people on my team do what I did in my business today?" He understands the power of duplication.)

Why was McDonald's exceptionally successful in the opening of thousands of new stores when expansion is the very thing that kills many growing businesses? There is one significant factor that explains this. Their duplication was successful because they had a **system**. And the genius of their system was its **simplicity**. Because their system was so simple, it could be consistently and successfully duplicated. (There was nothing complex about their original menu: soft drinks, shakes, one size of fries, and one type of burger!)

By keeping the business simple, they were able to establish a duplicable system which resulted in organizational depth. Collectively, each of these systems resulted in achievement of the corporate goal: massive revenue (wealth). Note that McDonald's achieved its original goal *by focusing on something else*: having a system that was simple and therefore duplicable. (In the business world you will often hear the expression "delegate or die"; its counterpart in network marketing is "duplicate or die".)

Let's look at the McDonald's process of opening a store in a linear form. Then we will compare this process to the growth of a network marketing business.

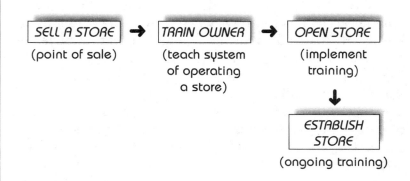

Admittedly, this is a very simplistic reduction of McDonald's process. But it is extremely illustrative to us in the growth of our businesses. McDonald's is involved in *the entire process* of selling a store/franchise, training the owners and personnel, opening the store, and then staying involved to ensure its ongoing success. In our network marketing business this is precisely what we must do.

Notice that the McDonald's corporation does not want to simply sell stores or franchises. They want to sell, open, and establish each store. If McDonald's didn't see the sale of each store/franchise as more than a "single point of transaction" all quality would slip. This is why they are committed to the ongoing success of each particular store. To ensure this success, they have a very specific system that teaches all of their personnel how to do their jobs.

Having a system that they teach, coupled with a commitment to the ongoing success of each store well beyond the point of sale, is what ensures McDonald's success in thousands of future sites. Through a well developed system that is successfully duplicated, they now have a worldwide customer base that trusts them to have a predictable and consistent level of quality and service. This creates satisfied customers along with a winning situation for the McDonald's corporation, shareholders, franchise owners, and employees.

Like McDonald's, Look Beyond "The Point of Sale"

This same process is applicable in network marketing. As leaders of growing teams we must see well beyond the point of sale (signing up new reps). Like McDonald's, we need to give new reps a system to plug into so they are set up for ongoing success. New reps, especially those who have no experience in network marketing, will look to us for direction. Having decided to get into the business, their thinking shifts to "What do I do with this business now that I am in it?" We need to give them direction and some tracks to run on, so that they know what to do with the very business we invited them to join us in.

Incidentally, as the industry of network marketing matures, it is attracting more people who view network

marketing as a very serious and significant means of transacting business. These individuals grow their businesses
with the same level of effort, patience, and professionalism that they would give to any other business endeavor.
They are not afraid of hard work; they are undaunted by
slow growth or disappointment, and they know what it is
to live in entrepreneurial time. These people did not select a network marketing company because they were
looking for a free ride or hoping to win the network mar-

> **"View each new rep
> that comes into your
> business as the
> equivalent of a new
> store or franchise."**

keting equivalent of the lottery. (That is, sponsoring a
rep who works the business with more vision, passion,
and success than the sponsor ever had. In turn the new
rep's success becomes a windfall for the upline sponsor.
This is luck, not leadership. It is financial gain, but not
personal achievement.)

This new era of network marketing is a welcome relief to the earlier days of the industry. Then, there was
too much hype, too many false expectations created, and
too little support given. There were too many people who
fancied themselves as business builders when in fact they
were nothing more than hustlers who viewed every prospect as a single point of sale. They took just enough time

with someone to talk them into joining their own business. Then they would take the money and run. This "slam-bam-thank you-mam" style had nothing to do with being a leader, growing a team, or being a serious business person. In its wake it left a large number of people who were turned off by the entire industry. As Richard Poe makes clear in his excellent books, those days are no longer the norm for our industry. This industry has increasingly high levels of integrity and sophistication. It is an emerging giant, and it is here to stay. Those individuals who grow their businesses by teaching their team a system that is duplicable will be the ones who experience the power of exponential growth and residual income in this industry.

While recognizing that McDonald's uses a system to ensure its ongoing success, some readers at this point will be thinking, "Tom, I have never really been trained. Consequently, I don't have any systematic way of growing my business. And I certainly don't have any systematic way of training my people. What do I do now?" These are excellent thoughts. The answer is less difficult than people anticipate. As leaders we need to give our team, especially new reps, tracks to run on.

TRACKS TO RUN ON

Do you remember a toy called the "slinky"? It is wire coiled into a circle that expands like an accordion. Slinkies are able to "flip" themselves down an entire flight of stairs. The objective is to hold the base of the slinky at the top of stairs and then flip the top half of the slinky over onto the next stair. As it lands on that stair, its momentum pulls on the remaining portion of the slinky and flips it onto the stair below. When successful, this process repeats itself all the way to the bottom of the stairs. What determines if the slinky makes it all the way to the bottom? It is the initial launch that determines its future success. If it has enough momentum and proper direction, then it is on its way.

Starting people correctly in a business can have this same result. If they begin with adequate momentum and proper direction, they are much more likely to stay on-task and become successful. This is why corporate leaders, like McDonald's, give their people "tracks to run on". Having "tracks" as guiderails helps people know, in very specific terms, what actions they need to take in their first hours, days, and weeks in the business.

The first hours and days in a new rep's business are vital. While enthusiasm may be high, confidence may be low. Beliefs are still forming, and commitment is, in all probability, still somewhat tentative. They are waiting to see if "this thing" will work for them. The less direction and assistance they have in their first hours and days, the more likely they are to get frustrated, bogged down, and tempted to quit.

Too many talented and well-meaning people stop working a business because they do not know what to do to get it going. Sadder still, are those who have not been given any tracks to run on. In a desire to get started, a rep may make earnest attempts to talk to others about his or her business, yet fail miserably. They make the common mistake of talking too much, listening too little, and being so overly enthusiastic that friends begin to wonder if the rep has been duped into joining some cult! This concern makes the friends not only avoid the business, but eager to talk the new rep out of it too! You can't blame a new rep for rethinking the whole situation after several of these experiences, which obscure vision, instill doubt, and dull enthusiasm. (I know of these mistakes because I made them so often in the early days of my business. I still make them occasionally.) Providing tracks to run on, along with upline support, minimizes these mistakes that are painful to newcomers and almost comical to network marketing veterans.

How to Know if You Are Providing "Tracks to Run on" for Your Team

Let me ask you a question. Suppose a new rep on your team comes to you as the upline leader and says, "I am new in the business, but I am completely available and teachable. What are the first ten things that you want me to understand and do?" Would you be able to pull out an *already printed* sheet of paper (not your company manual) with suggestions for the first actions they should take to successfully launch their new business? If you cannot do this there is a good chance people who join your team might not have tracks to run on. Creating this simple document could be the most important gift you, as a leader, can offer your team. The "tracks" that are developed will be different for each business. You will need to work with your rep when he or she addresses the items on the following list:

- Why am I getting into this business?
- What do I want out of my business?
- When will I host my first in-home meeting?
- What is the date of my first training session?
- Make a list of people's names and phone numbers to contact about my new business.
- When will I meet with my leader to begin calling the people on my list in three-way calls?
- * Essential materials that are necessary to successfully start my business.
- * Books, tapes, or videos to utilize
- * Instructions for printing business cards

* Miscellaneous forms that need to be filled out.

* Foundational principles the rep needs to grasp. (For instance, the three principles of network marketing or the four ingredients of success.)

(* Starred items should already be printed on the list you give your new rep.)

SUGGESTIONS FOR "TRACKS TO RUN ON"

Giving your team tracks to run on is helpful for several reasons:

1. It helps your new reps know what to do immediately upon entering the business. (This gives them purposeful direction which allows their enthusiasm to be harnessed while setting them up for prompt action and success.)

2. It increases your effectiveness as a leader. You are able to give reps very specific focus and action points.

3. It allows you to determine how serious reps are about the business.

4. It increases the likelihood of your reps' knowing how to lead and manage their own new reps because they can repeat what you did with them.

5. It creates an ongoing cycle of focus, action, quality, and results on your team.

When leaders design tracks to run on, it reduces their business to its simplest form and the most important action points. The result is significant. It will infuse your organization with "T.L.C." Not tender loving care. Rather, the ability to teach, lead, and coach.

TRACKS TO RUN ON ENABLE LEADERS TO EFFECTIVELY:	TEACH	LEAD	COACH

TRACKS TO RUN ON ENABLE LEADERS TO` DISCOVER WHO IS:	TEACH<u>ABLE</u>	LEAD<u>ABLE</u>	COACH<u>ABLE</u>

TRACKS TO RUN ON HELP LEADERS AND THEIR TEAMS KNOW WHAT TO DO NEXT.

Having tracks to run on equips leaders to diagnose reps' lack of growth. There are usually one or two explanations for reps' not having success in the early phase of their businesses. They may have no tracks to run on, or they have been given tracks to run on, but see no need for them.

When You Are So Good, You Are No Good

Ignoring the need for tracks to run on is the common malady for professionals getting into network marketing. They are convinced this business is easy, there is no real skill or science to it, and they know more about working with people and growing a business than their upline. Additionally, they are sure that they will quickly and effortlessly motivate all of their friends to join with them because of the compelling logic of their presentation.

This was the case with Bill. He was a professional who had enormous desire to succeed in his network marketing business. He had tremendous motivation, great experience in working with people, and he knew how to set goals and manage his time. He was a perfect candidate for this industry. Ironically, the same prodigious giftedness and experience that positioned him for success prevented him *from* success. His strengths were his liability. They made him unteachable. The proverbial loose cannon.

One evening, I was chatting with Bill on the phone to see how he was doing. I could hear his enthusiasm, desire, and longing to make his business grow. Equally, I could hear his growing frustration and doubt about the future of his business. Finally I simply told him,

"Bill, do you want to know what I think of when I listen to you? I know how much talent and desire your have. I know how gifted you are. You can run circles around most people in this industry. But you aren't, and you won't. You are like a locomotive engine that has an endless amount of raw power, energy, and potential. But with all of this ability you are going nowhere. The reason is because you are like a locomotive engine without tracks to run on. Consequently, you are completely bogged down in the mud. You are stuck. And you will stay stuck until you recognize the need for having a simple and systematic way of growing your business. Bill, when you decide to take all of your talent and harness it by putting the engine on the tracks, then you will begin to take off. Similarly, your team will stay bogged down until you give them simple tracks to run on. Like you, Bill, your team does not need motivation. It needs direction. Tracks to run on. When you start to use the tracks we have given you, your team will begin to rock and roll."

I was able to understand Bill's slow start because it was the same way I entered the world of network marketing. I entered overly confident, unaware of my ignorance, and clueless to the reality that there would be a learning curve in this industry just like any other major undertaking. This arrogance left me unteachable, and it precluded my understanding the need for simplicity in network marketing.

Initially, I attended meetings and felt embarrassed by their simplicity and pointed lack of "professionalism" as I knew it in the corporate world. I would sit in the audience and think, "If this person can make $70,000 per month with *that simple presentation,* what can I do when it is given more professionally?" I couldn't wait to get started. I didn't need help, teaching, or tracks to run on. I just needed everyone to get out of my way and let me get going. Being a self-starter, I took off and worked hard for a year. I could plan meetings, give presentations, and teach about my company better than most.

Eventually it dawned on me that I was working harder than most but not making any remarkable progress. Admitting my lack of significant success, I had to analyze the reason for it. I finally began to see my mistakes. My combination of experience, arrogance, and network marketing ignorance made me run my business so well that it was totally nonduplicable. I was so good that I was no good. Because what I did was not simple enough to be systematically duplicated. I had sensed the potential power of network marketing but missed seeing the invisible infrastructure that makes it work.

To use the McDonald's analogy, I was not positioning myself to be the CEO of McDonald's with thousands of stores/franchises. Rather, I was working as if I were the owner of one restaurant whose goal was to serve the fanciest and best burgers in my city. It finally occurred to me that I would rather be the network marketing equivalent of the CEO of McDonald's than the owner of one restaurant that serves fabulous burgers. With this realization, I finally began to see and teach the genius of simplicity and giving people tracks to run on. It has made all the difference in the world.

As you lead other professionals who join your team, don't be afraid to teach, lead and coach them. They need your help more than they know. Be honest with them; let them make their mistakes, and hope they are entrepreneurial enough to survive the learning curve in network marketing. Also, be aware that many professionals are not strong enough to make it in network marketing. After a few failures and rejections, many of them retreat back to their familiar work world. Because there, in their comfort zone, they have already mastered most of the learning curve. In this arena they can work for many days without experiencing any significant failure or rejection. They may be bored with their career, uninspired by their job, and just biding their time. But to them, tolerating this quiet boredom is more bearable than experiencing the initial self-doubt and mistakes that accompany any new learning curve. So they exchange the invitation of new dreams and challenges for the tepid waters of their daily work.

What to Do With Those Who Will Not Follow

Having specific, written tracks for new reps will give you a quick assessment of how teachable and motivated they are. You will quickly discover if they are motivated entrepreneurs or just "talkers". When I go over the "tracks to run on" that I use in my business, I tell people, "I will know in 48 hours if you are serious about this business." The reason for this is obvious: If they will not take the simple, initial steps necessary to launch their businesses when their motivation is high and their vision is clear, then they are probably not going to take them when they get immersed in all the other important details of their daily lives. As a rule of thumb, most people who start slow in this business stay slow. (There are exceptions to this. For example, some people enter our businesses at a time when their schedules are already full. These people may be completely committed to growing their new business but they need time for their schedules to clear before they can get seriously involved.)

Inevitably, we will have people join our business who then do nothing with it. Psychologically, this is, to me, one of the most intriguing and fascinating dimensions of this industry. But practically, as business builders, we need to know what to do with those who will not follow. Following are some suggestions:

- *Be patient with them in the beginning.* Over time, as their belief level rises, their involvement may too.

- *Be honest and direct with them.* Tell them you are willing to help them but you cannot want this business for them more than they want it for themselves.

- *Go sponsor someone else.* Don't put your business on hold while you wait for someone to get moving.

- *Notify them of group events.* But don't give them your individual time. Give your best time to those who demonstrate they are serious about their business.

- *Let them go.* Your success is not contingent on them. Work with someone who is motivated and teachable.

- *Be gracious to them.* There are numerous factors that prevent people from pursuing their own desires.

- *Stop trying to resurrect the dead.* That is a very limited specialty. Besides, you are running a business, not a mission.

Without question, leading the people on a growing team is one of the most challenging and rewarding dimensions of this industry. This task is made immeasurably easier if we remember that leadership is providing vision, skill, and motivation.

LEADERSHIP IS PROVIDING VISION, SKILL, AND MOTIVATION

Did you ever go into a restaurant and order one menu item and then have the waiter bring you something totally different? It is annoying not to get what you anticipated. This same "mix up" often occurs in network marketing. As your team develops, be careful not to confuse your team members' selections. If you listen carefully, they will let you know what they want or need. They may not come out and say it, but you will *sense* it if you pay attention to their words, attitudes, and actions. You will discover that their menu selections often fall into the three categories that leaders can provide.

| VISION | SKILL | MOTIVATION |

These are three aspects of what leaders can provide to those whom they lead. Simultaneously, they are the three primary ingredients necessary for reps to sustain focus in the development of a business.

It is a winning combination when a team leader gives people on the team precisely what they need. When this happens regularly, there is an ongoing sense of working together, staying on-task, and strong momentum. Conversely, when it doesn't happen, things begin to feel out of sync, and momentum starts to stall. If you examine the most successful network marketing companies, or the most successful groups within a particular company, you will discover that they each provide a rich mixture of vision, skill, and motivation.

In leading those on your team, be sure that your repertoire of responses to people can at least address these three categories. Some people in positions of leadership are like a "one trick pony". No matter what happens, they have only one response, answer, or piece of advice to give to others. Over time, these responses are not useful to the rep who was hoping for some substantive insight or encouragement. They are only helpful to the person who gives the response because it gives them the illusion of having dealt with the issue at hand. We need more than glib answers or trite responses to those who are looking to us as a catalyst for their own commitment. Knowing what combination of vision, skill, or motivation someone needs enables us to do this.

Let's examine what each of these provide.

VISION: It allows people to envision the future. It is a sneak preview of potential realities for those who stay on-task. It is seeing the big picture or, the macro-view, of things to come. It is knowing with certainty what will occur tomorrow if we are diligent today.

The power of vision is its ability to give people hope and direction. It can infuse people with the will to work today because they can see how today's efforts will bring them incrementally closer to what they see and want in the future. The more clearly someone sees the future, the more confidently they work in the present. This is because, to them, the future is so real, close, and palpable that it overrides whatever minor hassles may be encountered today. In short, clarity of vision is what keeps entrepreneurs living in a resource state instead of a problem state. It is what keeps them feeling strong and upbeat rather than significantly discouraged.

In any business there are stretches of road where nothing seems to be falling into place. People can be working hard and doing things well but not seeing immediate results or success. This same thing happens periodically in a network marketing business. In these moments, vision is a vital ingredient. Those who have it can get twenty five rejections in a row and not be the least bit shaken. Why? Because those with clear vision barely notice the people who said "no" to their business. They are already focused on those twenty-five in the future who will say "yes" and then duplicate themselves into thousands of others. This future reality keeps reps so confident and excited that they genuinely don't mind when some say "no" to their business in the present.

SKILL: This is expertise, proficiency, and competence. It is not only knowing what to do, but how to do it as well. It is practical knowledge applied in the daily development of a network marketing business. Skill can be acquired and developed, and it is imperative for success in our business.

As leaders, we need to keep in mind that many people lose heart in their new networking businesses, not because they lack vision, commitment, or motivation. They lose heart because they get tired of failure. They grow weary of "striking out". To put this in context, imagine what it would be like to be a major league baseball player. Initially, that would sound pretty exciting to many people. But if you were a major league player who struck out every time you were at bat, eventually you would begin to dread game days instead of look forward to them. In those times you would not need a pep talk. You would need a batting coach. Because the root issue would be your swing flaws, not your drive or desire. If this could be corrected, your attitude and motivation would be fine.

> *"...don't assume that people understand the most basic aspects of growing their businesses."*

When you interact with reps who are not successful in having others join their business, be thoughtful about what you say to them. Instead of telling them to "hang in there" or reminding them that "this business is a numbers game" you might want to ask them a question. Gently ask, "Can you tell me what you say to people when you ask them if they would like to learn more about your business?" Be prepared to be appalled at the answers you will hear. I have been shocked at some of the answers I have heard to this question. At that point, I usually tell the rep, "If that is what you shared with me, I would not want to look at your business either. Would you like some assistance in talking to others?"

Don't assume that people understand the most basic aspects of growing their business because they are a professional, or have been to some form of training, or watched you model how to dialogue with others. They need to repeatedly be taught, modeled to, assisted, launched on their own, and then evaluated and assisted some more. While we like to keep our business very simple, the skills required to effectively interact with others are far more subtle and complex than you may recognize.

Have you ever seen the show *Home Improvement* starring Tim Allen? He regularly goes to "Wilson," his neighbor across the fence, for advice. Wilson always gives him clear and succinct counsel. Afterwards, Tim attempts to communicate what he has just heard to someone else. Invariably, he completely mangles the message, and the meaning of what he heard! His words are not even remotely close to what Wilson said! This same thing happens regularly in our business. People can be well supported and trained. Then, when they are on their own, they completely forget or ignore all that they were taught. This business that appeared so easy is now beginning to look impossible to them. They are getting discouraged. But what they need from their upline leadership are skills, along with fresh vision and motivation.

MOTIVATION: This is a great quality. It is drive, desire, and determination. It is the fire in the belly that makes someone want to stay on-task. It is the reason for people to do something new or different. It is the fuel source that helps them sustain focus.

Motivation has two sources. One is internal, and the other is external. The most profound and lasting is motivation that comes from within the individual rep. Reps who tap into their own private wellspring of personal motivation are those who are rarely stopped. They know what they want and why they want it. Knowing the "what" and the "why" of their businesses creates the drive to chase their dreams. It gives them the will to work. This is why one of the first things a leader does with a new rep is clarify the four ingredients of success. When these are clearly identified, they can be used by the new rep for his or her own internal motivation or by the upline leader to provide external motivation.

As a leader, be a student of those you lead. If you listen carefully, they will indicate what mixture of insight they need from you in the areas of vision, skill, and motivation. Correct diagnosis makes it much easier to find useful solutions in the arena of leadership.

> *"The more clearly someone sees the future the more confidently they work in the present."*

What If I Have Never Been in a Leadership Position Before?

As I stated at the beginning of this section on leadership, give yourself permission to grow as a leader. Don't worry if you have never had a leadership position or title before. And don't worry about what title or position you hold in your particular network marketing company. *Remember that leadership by influence is far more powerful than leadership by title or position.* The world of network marketing, just like the corporate and political world, is full of people with impressive sounding leadership titles or positions who are not leaders at all. And they are regularly overshadowed by dear men and women who have genuine influence and impact on those around them. If you doubt this, look at the lives of Mother Teresa and Princess Diana They were leaders by virtue of their influence, not their titles. While growing your business, if you should get lost along the road of leadership, just remember their example: be a servant, honestly care about others, and commit yourself to what you believe in.

CHAPTER
TWELVE

IT'S GAME TIME

In the growth of my business I often explain to people that I am the equivalent of a player/coach in the NFL. As a player, I am out there doing what every one else is. I study, work hard, take my shots, and continually look for occasions to articulate to others my excitement and confidence in network marketing and in the particular company with which I affiliated. In my role as a coach, I am committed to helping others understand how to succeed in this industry.

On game day, a coach wants to leave a few final thoughts in the forefront of his players' minds. He knows he only has a few moments left before the opening kick-off. After that, the ball is literally in his players' hands. It is now up to the players to execute. It is their turn to get started, stay focused, play hard, and make their desire for a win become a reality.

In effect, that is where we are now in this book. We are in the last chapter, the home stretch. It is game time. It is time for me to get out of the way and for you take the ball and run with it. It is your move. It is your moment to take your dreams, your life, and your future and start to run with them. As a coach who has both pride and confidence in his team, let me share a few last thoughts with you.

Congratulations

First, allow me to congratulate you for your tenacity. There are many people who rarely purchase or read a book. Others purchase them but never quite get around to reading them. Still others begin a book but never finish it. But you have finished what you started. You kept going... one word, one page, one chapter at a time. (Even though there were probably some portions of the book that you enjoyed more than others.) The act of continuing what you began has put you at the finish line.

If you will take this same behavior and apply it to your business, it will create the same result. Your dreams and goals will become reality. Remember, the most surprising aspect of success in life is not how difficult and elusive it is, it is how deceptively simple it is. Success most frequently visits those who dare to dream, then take a series of small, incremental steps every day in pursuit of their dream.

In theory, when they stop to think about it, most people agree with the simplicity of success. However, in reality, they never quite get around to applying this concept in their lives *now*. Today. How many people do you know who, for years, have talked about what they were going to do? But they never get around to actually doing what they have been talking and dreaming about. There is always a reason why *today* is not quite the right time.

They are endlessly on the verge of beginning to "get ready" to get started. Somehow the first serious steps in the pursuit of their dreams are never taken. Over time, others begin to recognize that these people don't truly have a dream. They are just dreamers. They are wishers. Sometimes they are whiners. But they are not workers pursuing a dream. Consequently, they will never be winners.

> "Today is the only day you can shape, manage, and control."

Having read this far, you are not merely a dreamer. You have a dream. You are an entrepreneur at heart. (This is true, even if you never knew or admitted it before reading this book.) As you get ready to "take the ball and run," remember that *today* is the only day you can shape, manage, and control. Peter Drucker is correct when he says, "The best way to predict the future is to create it." Break away from the vast majority of people who endlessly delay the pursuit of their dreams one day at a time. Separate yourself from those who make procrastination an art. Adopt the motto, "PROCRASTINATE LATER!" Realize today is a gift and that you intend to use it to shape your future. Don't be lulled into inaction by thinking that "commitment is just around the corner."

COMMITMENT: IT IS JUST AROUND THE CORNER!

Many people live their entire lives with the soothing misconception that "commitment is just around the corner." In the very near future, they tell themselves, they are going to get started on what they purport to be a high priority for them. (This could be losing weight, getting into shape, learning a new skill, starting a new business or hobby, improving their relationships, etc.) As time goes on, they never "turn the corner" and get started. It is as if their life is a long, continuous bend in the road that never ends! However, by telling themselves that they will soon get started, they get to "have their cake and eat it too." They have the momentary satisfaction of imagined future achievement while being able to avoid all the immediate work and effort that are necessary in the present. Initially, this can seem like a pretty good strategy. But over time, it begins to feel very hollow. In the privacy of their own minds they know that talk is cheap.

You can avoid this costly pattern of letting your life slip away one day at a time if you will think of your life span as segments of time. Let's say that the average person will live a productive life for eighty years. This means that you can break your life down into eight decades. Now imagine each decade as a "chit" that you get to play in the game of life. We all have about eight chits that we get to use or invest as we want.

Normally, two of these chits are used just getting us ready for our productive years. That is to say, most of us spend about two decades getting ready for our adult lives. That leaves six chits left to play. Next, factor in your age. How many more chits has that taken? For many entrepreneurs, realizing they have just a handful of chits to play in life motivates them to enjoy and use each day to its fullest. As a result, their daily lives are rich with purpose and focus.

How many chits do you have left to invest in the game of life? Focus on those you have left, not on those you have used. How do you want to invest those that remain? Clarify your dreams, set some goals, and take the next step necessary to achieve your goals and dreams...today. It is time to turn the corner, be committed, and get going. Your dreams, just like your life, are simultaneously your privilege and responsibility to manage. Once you accept this reality, it sets you free to take hold of the future rather than passively sitting around and wondering what the future holds.

TRAVEL TIPS WHILE PURSING YOUR DREAM

INERTIA: WINNING THE DAILY BATTLE

Do you remember the definition of "inertia" from your high school or college physics class? Part of the definition usually states that "an object at rest tends to remain at rest." This law of science has applications far beyond the world of physics. It is a common reality of daily life impacting our attitudes, decisions, and actions.

While you pursue your dream and grow your business, inertia will tempt you to "remain at rest." It will weave a spell that makes inactivity and procrastination seem like the most plausible and rational course of action. This temptation, while always present, is remarkably subtle. It will never ask you to blatantly abandon your aspirations. Rather, it quietly suggests that activity and exertion be forestalled *only for the moment*. Certainly what is important today can be acted upon tomorrow without any serious impact on one's future and life. So, ignoring what needs to be done, countless people succumb to the comfort of what is immediately attractive. Over time, the daily, habitual capitulation to comfort and inertia will cause their dreams and lives to slip away one decision, one moment, one day at a time.

Recently, I saw the subtle power of inertia and its ability to immobilize even the most gifted and motivated people. Carol, who is on my team, had not been actively involved in anything we were doing for a number of weeks. I was curious about this because I knew she had a dream and that she was one of the most capable people on my team. (As a leader, I wanted to help her; as a clinician I wanted her to understand what was going on inside of her; as a researcher I wanted to grasp why motivated people sometimes mysteriously fade away in this industry.) So I called her to gently inquire about her inactivity. Her answer was succinct, honest, and powerful. She simply stated, "Tom, I did not quit. I just stopped." Bang! Inertia had claimed another victim. At the scene of the crime there was no sign of forced entry or struggle. Her dream was intact; her confidence was high, and her beliefs in the power of network marketing were strong. But inertia, working like a drug that leaves the mind intact while paralyzing the body, had claimed another victim. She was rendered immobile. And it happened with such insidious subtlety that she never knew what hit her.

Learning to overcome the initial allure of inertia and inactivity will allow you to enjoy the satisfaction of achievement and success. The more you experience this satisfaction, the easier it becomes to win the battle against inertia. This is because productivity and victory are inherently energizing. They infuse you with energy, motivation, and drive, which propel you to further action.

Success and energy do not begin working for you until you win the daily battle of overcoming "initial inertia." Sometimes the most difficult part of any endeavor, even those we enjoy, is simply getting started. For example, for years I have enjoyed cross training. Running and weight training are a regular part of my life. Years ago I identified the most difficult part of my workout. It is not running four or five miles or pushing myself beyond my limits in the weight room. *The hardest part of working out is tying my shoes!* Getting started is a daily battle, even when it is something that I enjoy and know is good for me. Once I get started, I am absolutely delighted that I made the right decision and won the battle again.

In growing your business, accept the reality that dealing with inertia is a fact of life. It is a reality that will never go away and a battle that must be won over and over. Make the decision to let your life dreams and goals be the deciding factors in the management of your daily life.

PART-TIME DOES NOT EQUAL PARTIAL QUALITY

One of the most wonderful aspects of network marketing is the freedom to grow a business on a part-time basis. Rarely can people find a business that has such extraordinary potential while being able to accommodate each participant's schedule. As we previously noted, you can work your business full-time and you can work your business part-time. But you cannot work it "spare time" because none of us have any. We have been using it up every day of our lives. Additionally, don't expect your business to create the equivalent of full-time income while you only work it on a part-time basis. This is not likely to occur until a significant period of time has been invested in your business.

While keeping these thoughts in mind, realize that part-time does not mean partial quality. Imagine working part-time for someone else in a traditional business setting. Let's say that you were only working twenty hours per week. Even though you would only be working half-time (half of a forty-hour work week), your employers would not expect a fifty percent reduction in your work quality. They would expect you to produce high quality work on a part-time basis.

Be sure to expect the same thing of yourself in the growth of your business. Don't let the luxury of being your own boss and setting your own goals and work schedule become a license to sloppy work or diminished quality. In network marketing, "simple" does not mean easy. Nor does simple mean a lesser commitment to excellence. When working your business, do it to the best of your current ability. Whether you are making phone calls, doing a business presentation, or training someone on your team, work your business with enthusiasm that is matched with excellence. It is an attractive combination that reflects well on you, your business, and our industry as a whole.

LIFE HAPPENS

Do you recall a bumper sticker several years ago that simply stated, "*!#&* happens?" Its sardonic humor mixed with truth made it somewhat popular. While noting the bumper sticker, I always felt it was incomplete. It should have said, "*!#&* happens. But don't take it personally."

While working hard and growing your business, things will happen that are less than fun. Without question, there will be moments when your business is not growing as fast as you wish; people will not be as motivated as you think is appropriate, and other things will occur that can erode your immediate joy. In these moments don't interpret what is happening as something that is being uniquely visited upon you. Be careful not to take the normal frustrations of growing your business *personally*, as if others are exempt from what you are experiencing.

In network marketing, individuals who have never before started or owned a business are often most susceptible to these erroneous conclusions when times get tough. This is because they have no frame of reference to which they can compare their experience. They do not know that fatigue, frustration, or fear are the occasional but normal experience of every entrepreneur in the pursuit of a dream.

Sometimes people who are new to network marketing misunderstand what they are experiencing in the growth of their business. Occasionally, they have been lied to by others concerning what it takes to succeed in this business. (Or, they misunderstood what they heard from others.) For instance, have you ever heard anyone say, "There is no sweat to this business." Or, have you heard them comment that "this business is so easy" while laughing about sleeping in and getting up late each morning. Only one of several things can be true when people say things like this. If they claim to be sleeping late, never breaking a sweat, and finding this business easy, they are: a) lying; b) telling the truth but making no money; or c) telling the truth in that they *currently* are able to sleep late while finding the business easy and no sweat because they *previously* paid their dues in the growth of their business. Now they are honestly enjoying the fruits of their courage, hard work, and tenacity. The power of network marketing and residual income is working for them because they worked their business.

Remember What Is "Normal"

While I was gathering data for this chapter, my wife and I went out to dinner with some of our dearest friends. In this couple, both the husband and the wife are macroentrepreneurs. Each of them knows what it is to conceive, start, and grow a large successful corporation. During dinner I asked the husband about the present business he is running. Several years and millions of dollars have already been invested in this start-up company, which is in the process of going public. On that very day he had received word from the Securities and Exchange Commission that his IPO would be delayed by one month. This simple delay, which seemed so innocuous to the SEC, meant this man would have to reach into his own pocket and write another check for one hundred thousand dollars.

The next time you are frustrated with some aspect of your business, remind yourself that you are not alone. Difficult moments are a normal part of life in any significant endeavor. And they are most certainly a normal part of growing any business. You will either get through them or done in by them. Tough times have to be endured if triumph is going to be enjoyed. Remember, there is a reason that you, as an entrepreneur, are worth every dollar that comes to you in the end. You will be paid not just for your time or your talent. More importantly, you will be paid for daring to dream, for raw courage, and for unyielding faith. The sum total of these rare qualities is what qualifies you to receive extraordinary returns in revenue and personal satisfaction in the end.

PICK A HORSE AND RIDE IT

Have you ever gone to the circus and seen one of the circus performers ride two horses at the same time? While it is entertaining to watch, none of us would consider simultaneously riding two horses as a serious means of transportation.

The same thing holds true in network marketing. If you intend to use this wonderful industry as a means of transportation, i.e. getting you from point "A" (where you are in life) to point "B" (where you want to go in life) then you will have to "pick a horse and ride it." I do not believe that you can be actively involved in several different network marketing companies if you intend to be a serious business builder. You don't have enough time, passion, or energy to disperse in multiple directions.

On one hand, I think people get involved with multiple companies because they enjoy the vast array of high quality products and services available in our industry. This is fine. But others get involved in multiple companies because they keep looking for the proverbial free lunch. They are looking for a "free ride" to financial free-

> "Your dreams, just like your life, are simultaneously your privilege and responsibility to manage."

dom. And they are certain if they can just hitch their wagon to the right company or individual, they will be able to generate serious residual income with minimal effort. As a result, they are involved with multiple companies. Or, they abandon one company to embrace another, certain that the new company will require less work while yielding swifter and higher returns.

(Regrettably, there still exists a small percentage of people in this industry who love to prey on others who have naive expectations. They are quick to promise these dear people that if they will sign up with their companies, and especially their teams, then indeed there will be the "opportunity" to get in on "explosive growth" wherein they can make far more money, in shorter periods of time, with far less effort, etc. etc. In my mind, these individuals, who are less prevalent in this new era of network marketing, are neither entrepreneurs nor business builders. They are more like modern day pirates who sail in, sell hype, rob downlines, and move on.)

So while growing your business, stay rooted in reality. The invitation to affiliate with a network marketing company is not an opportunity (a word that I use as infrequently as possible in my business) to do little and reap much. Rather, it is an invitation to use this industry, along with the company you have selected, as an arena in which you can chase your dreams. It is an invitation to dream big, grow a business, mature as a person, lead a team, touch the lives of others, and work harder than you have ever worked before. The byproduct, over time, can be residual income that gives you financial freedom that most others cannot even imagine, let alone experience.

If you are currently involved with a network marketing company and you trust the company's leadership, like its products/services, the compensation potential, and have passion for what you are doing, then stay put. Ride this horse for all it is worth. Get comfortable in the saddle and keep going. Focus on the destination and continue plodding ahead.

DON'T LET ANYONE STEAL YOUR DREAMS

Have you ever gone camping and used a Coleman lantern? One of the most interesting parts of the lantern is the mantle, which becomes extremely fragile after it has been lit. If bumped too hard, it will disintegrate. But when properly cared for and fueled, a mantle gives off an amazing amount of light. Our dreams are like this. They are as fragile as Coleman lantern mantles. But an intact dream, when properly fueled and cared for, gives enormous light. Protecting the dream is your responsibility. Be careful not to let others damage or steal it.

Remember, as an entrepreneur, you have the increasing ability to see things that many others cannot see. As you grow your business and associate with other entrepreneurs, you will develop 2/500 vision. You will be capable of effortlessly seeing at five hundred feet what others cannot see at a distance of two feet. Do not let the inability of others to see what is immediately in front of them cause you to doubt the reality of your own vision. Be thankful for your vision, grateful for a dream, and unshakable in your determination to make what you see in your mind's eye real in your experience. Lastly, remember that you are stronger than you know.

YOU ARE STRONGER THAN YOU KNOW

In my work over the years I have had the pleasure of interacting with some of the most remarkable individuals in the world from all walks of life (political, corporate, media, entertainment, and professional sports). There is, however, one individual who stands out in my mind as being the most interesting human being whom I have ever met. Her name is Susan Butcher. I admire her for the clarity of her dream and her willingness to do whatever it takes to be her best. She is a world class musher, which means she races dog sleds. As a musher, she holds nine speed records. Four times she has won one of the most grueling tests of skill, courage, and stamina ever conceived in the history of competition. She races in the Iditerod. It is a race held each year on the first Saturday in March; it begins in Anchorage, Alaska, and continues over eleven hundred miles to Nome, Alaska.

Susan told me the story of one of her recent Iditerod races. She was in the lead with only forty miles to go. At this point, another musher finally caught up with her, and then he passed her. She wanted to press on and re-take the lead but she was too tired. Total exhaustion had taken its toll, and fatigue had become her dominant reality. Her focus began to slip, and she began to compromise her dream. She told herself that coming in second would be okay. She found brief comfort in conceding first place and yielding to her fatigue. It would be so much easier...

But then, briefly, amazingly, her mind cleared. She remembered what she truly wanted: victory. She recalled the words of an old Alaskan sage who had told her, "There are many hard things in life. But there is only one sad thing: quitting." Heroically, she began to manage her thoughts and emotions rather than letting them manage her. Suddenly she dug deeper into her inner strength than she had ever dug before. She told herself,

"I did not spend nearly two weeks racing in forty degrees below zero weather with only two hours of sleep per night to come in second place!"

"I did not travel over ten thousand miles via dog sled this year to prepare for this race in order to come in second place!"

"I did not breed, raise, and train one hundred and fifty dogs to come in second place!"

"I did not feed my dogs five times per day and take five to seven different teams of dogs out every day to come in second place!"

"I did not just race over four mountain ranges, one hundred and seventy miles of ocean, and one hundred and fifty miles on the Yukon River to come in second place!"

"I have dreamed and trained and worked to be a winner!"

With a will to win that was unflinching, she got off of her sled and ran the last forty miles. In the process she recaptured the lead and won the race.

Now it is your turn. It is game time. As a coach, I have only one last thing to say to you. Dare to dream and work to win.